I0142868

A Theological Journey . . .

insights on the faith once delivered

# A Theological Journey . . .

## insights on the faith once delivered

Gordon T. Borden, M.Ed., M.A.R.

Ekklesia Publications
Frisco, Texas
2016

A Theological Journey . . .
*insights on the faith once delivered*

ISBN 0-9904282-6-5
© Gordon T. Borden, M.Ed., M.A.R.

EKKLESIA

Published by
Ekklesia Society
P. O. BOX 5343
Frisco, Texas 75035

Printed in the United States of America

Unless otherwise noted, Scripture taken from the New King James Version ®.
Copyright © 1982 by Thomas Nelson, Inc. Used by permission. All rights reserved

ALL RIGHTS RESERVED

No portion of this book may be reproduced, stored in a retrieval system, or transmitted in any form or by any means, including electronic, mechanical, photocopying, recording, or otherwise, without prior permission from the author or publisher. The only exception is brief quotes in printed reviews.

For all book orders:
www.ekk.org
or
www.amazon.com

this book is dedicated to

Holden

the grandson of my later years

# TABLE OF CONTENTS

CHAPTER SEVEN

**MINIMAL VS. EXPLICIT ARTICULATIONS OF THE FAITH: A COMPARISON OF THE ARTICLES OF RELIGION AND THE BELGIC CONFESSION**

# ACKNOWLEDGEMENTS

As noted in the Preface, the chapters in this book are the product of studies I taught at several churches and courses I undertook at Cranmer Theological House. I am grateful for the outstanding leadership and teaching provided at that institution, which is committed to "rightly dividing the Word of truth" and to encouraging students in their academic pursuits. I thank each of the individuals who taught and challenged us to dig deep into the Scriptures and to commit ourselves to being "workmen who need not be ashamed." I am also very grateful for the encouragement of my wife, the Rev. Dr. B. Lee Ligon-Borden, who still claims I'm the smartest person she ever met (and I just let her continue in that fantasy, as she's very happy with it) and has been my champion through numerous challenges. I present this work to the next generations as a testimony to the faithfulness of God in my life and in the lives of those who love me and those who taught me.

# PREFACE

Theology, once considered an honored study receives little recognition today, other than occasional boredom or scorn. Certainly, the lack of interest in theology (the study of God and His work) aligns with the neglect of Holy Scripture as a guide for daily life. The term "Christian" is tossed about indiscriminately, as was clear from the claims of candidates for the highest office of the land during the 2016 debate debacle. Seminaries, once the fount of theological studies, report increasing, even incremental, decline in the number of applicants, with the accompanying tendency to accept students who would not have been considered in decades past. The so-called "dumbing-down" of the applicant pool has led to the decline in academic standards, as it has in public schools and even colleges and universities. Hence, seminaries pump out individuals ill-equipped to share their faith in Christ, if they even have come to that point in their spiritual journey, and barely aware of the nuances of Scripute. Indeed, one priest commented that he made it through four years of seminary (at a well-respected seminary) without ever cracking a Bible. His faith in Christ and his hunger for God's Word came years later.

So where does that leave us? I'm suggesting we start with the term Christian – a follower of Jesus Christ, the promised Messiah, the Son of the living God. Apart from a relationship with Him, one simply is not a Christian, regardless of the creed or liturgy one may espouse. As a Christian, one should not only be in relationship with God through faith in Jesus Christ but also be a follower, a disciple, one who does the bidding of his master, the Lord Jesus. That realization, of course, takes us to the Scriptures, where we learn of the life of Christ, find His teachings, and receive the teachings of His apostles, as well as all the beautiful messages that preceded His advent, namely what we call the "Old Covenant."

I am not providing a commentary or theology textbook here, so if the reader is looking for either, another source should be sought. Rather, after many years of biblical studies and ten years in seminary, attending as a "returning student" (a euphemism for an "old coot") part-time while engaged as a headmaster of a private school for at-risk youth, I am offering some insights I gained from studies under exceptional scholars. Because I had the privilege of sitting under these wise individuals and have been encouraged (under some duress!), to share insights I gained from that experience, I am putting together a selection of thoughts, if you will, that I hope will serve to honor the Lord Jesus and speak to some of his disciples who do not have the advantage of going to seminary but long to know more about Him. These are my thoughts, so any fault that may be found in them lies with me, certainly not the astute academicians who taught me.

And, so, we begin…..

Gordon T. Borden, M.Ed., M.A.R.
Spring, Texas
April, 2016

# Chapter One

## JESUS CHRIST
### The Implications of the Person of Christ
### In His Work and in the Sacraments

John Stott, in his book *Life in Christ*, writes that Paul in one brief paragraph (Romans 5:1-11) repeats the preposition "through" five times. He explains that "through the death of Christ we are reconciled to God, that we obtain access into the state of grace, that we enjoy peace with God, and that we rejoice in God."[1] All of the blessings are bestowed on us because of Christ's sacrifice and the ongoing mediation of Christ on our behalf. In John 14:6, Christ proclaimed, "I am the way, the truth, and the life. No one comes to the Father except through Me." From eternity past, during the time that Christ walked amongst us, and until the end of the ages, His work continues. While He walked amongst us, He took on human form, and today, in His resurrection and ascension, He continues to "walk amongst us" but in a different capacity.

### Christ's Person and Work on Earth

*In the beginning was the Word, and the Word was with God,*
*and the Word was God …. and the Word became flesh and dwelt amongst us, and*
*we beheld His glory, glory as of the only begotten of the Father, full of grace and truth.*
*(John 1:1-14)*

Jesus Christ's work in his incarnation – when He walked amongst us -- is seen in the hypostatic union – the union of God with man. Basic orthodox doctrine established by the Council of Chalcedon (451 A.D.) speaks of Christ's two natures, one and the same Christ, Son, Lord, only begotten to be acknowledged in two natures, unchangeably, indelibly, inseparably; the distraction of natures being by no means taken away by the union, but rather the property of each nature being preserved, and

---

[1] Stott, John. *Life in Christ*. Eastbourne: Kingsway; Wheaton, IL: Tyndale House, 1991, p . 6, and cited in Stott, John. *Authentic Christianity*. Ed. Timothy Dudley-Smith. Downers Grove, IL: InterVarsity, Press, 1995, p. 57

concurring in one Person and one Substance (hypostasis), not parted or divided into two persons, but one and the same Son, the only begotten, God of the Word, the Lord Jesus Christ, as the prophets from the beginning [have declared] concerning him, and the Lord Jesus Christ himself has taught us and the Creed of the holy Fathers has handed down to us.[2]

> In becoming man, the second Person of the Godhead did not cease to be God; He did not give up his divinity. If He had, he would have needed salvation himself.

In speaking about Christ's work on earth, the well-known Anglican writer J. I. Packer talks about Jesus' fulfillment of the Father's redemptive will.[3] The first stage of the Father's purpose was humiliation. In this stage, Jesus let go of his glory through the incarnation, living as a poor man, a religious outsider, and a condemned criminal dying on the cross as the sin-bearer of mankind. Perhaps the most succinct and best known passage regarding the hypostatic union is found in Paul's letter to the Philippians, in which he explains that Christ Jesus,

> who, being in the form of God, did not consider it robbery to be equal with God, but made Himself of no reputation, taking the form of a bondservant, and coming in the likeness of men. And being found in appearance as a man, He humbled Himself and became obedient to the point of death, even the death of the cross.[4]

In becoming man, the second Person of the Godhead did not cease to be God; He did not give up his divinity. If He had, he would have needed salvation himself. Stott notes that Christ "was neither God pretending to be human, nor a human being with divine faculties, nor semi-divine and semi-human, but fully human and fully divine, the unique God-man.[5]

---

[2] Shaff, Phillips, *The Creeds of Christendom*. New York: Harper and Brothers, 1919, Vol 2, p. 62 quoted by Millard Erickson in Introducing Christian Doctrine. Ed. L. Arnold Hustad. Grand Rapids, MI:Baker Book House, 1992

[3] Packer, J. I. *Concise Theology: A Guide to Historic Christian Beliefs*. Wheaton, IL: Tyndale House Publishers, Inc.,1993, p.119-120

[4] Philippians 2:6-8

[5] Stott, John. *The Incomparable Christ*. Downers Grove, IL: InterVarsity Press, 2001, p. 85

Macleod explains that the term 'hypostatic union' encapsulates three truths: that Christ is one person; that the union between his two natures arises from the fact that they both belong to one and the same person; and that this one person, the son of God, is the Agent behind all of the Lord's actions, the Speaker of all his utterances and the Subject of all his experiences.[6] . . .

Part of the Anglican tradition is to proclaim as part of the liturgy the orthodox position as elucidated in the Nicene Creed, which refutes heresies to the contrary and succinctly states the aspects of the hypostatic union:

> We believe in one Lord, Jesus Christ, the only Son of God, eternally begotten of the Father, God from God, Light from Light, true God from true God, begotten, not made, of one Being with the Father . . . . by the power of the Holy Spirit he became incarnate from the Virgin Mary, and was made man.

In becoming human, He took on all the characteristics of humanity, but without sin. In His humanity, Christ Jesus experienced the joys and travails of humanity. He enjoyed times with His disciples, He ate, He slept, He prayed, and He struggled with Satan's temptations. Macleod describes his human nature in this way: "He was born, baptized, tempted and transfigured. He beheld the city and wept over it. He agonized in Gethsemane. He was betrayed, arrested and condemned He was flogged, immolated, crucified, dead and buried."[7]

Furthermore, if He had not been completely human, He could not have understood our condition and identified with our temptations. Hebrews 4:15 says that "we do not have a High Priest who cannot sympathize with our weaknesses, but was in all points tempted as we are, yet without sin."

In his death, the God-man Jesus Christ bore our sins in His own body and purchased our redemption. John wrote that "the blood of Jesus Christ his Son cleanseth us from all sin."[8]

---

[6]  Macleod, Donald. *The Person of Christ: Contours of Christian Theology*. Downers Grove, IL: InterVarsity Press, 1998, p. 189
[7]  Macleod, p. 189-190
[8]  I John 1:7

The second stage was His exaltation—His resurrection, ascension, and position with The Father. In the Nicene Creed, we proclaim that Jesus Christ "rose from the dead, ascended into heaven, and sits at the right hand of the Father." Peter, when he answered the charge of the high priests, told them that "The God of our fathers raised up Jesus, whom you murdered by hanging on a tree. Him God has exalted to His right hand *to be* Prince and Savior, to give repentance to Israel and forgiveness of sins."[9] He is now seated at the right hand of God, where He reigns as the eternal King over the world and the Church, and from which he sends the Holy Spirit according to his promise that

> But when the Helper comes, whom I shall send to you from the Father, the Spirit of truth who proceeds from the Father, He will testify of Me. And you also will bear witness, because you have been with Me from the beginning.[10]

Our redemption does not end with His death or even His resurrection because even today Christ draws us to Himself. He intercedes on our behalf, guards, guides, and cares for us like a shepherd cares for his flock.[11] In the *Book of Common Prayer* of the Anglican Church, we attest to Christ's continued work on our behalf in the Holy Communion prayer in which we simply state that "If any man sin, we have an Advocate with the Father, Jesus Christ the righteous; and he is the Propitiation for our sins."[12]

## Christ's Person in The Sacraments

Christ's exaltation enables Him in a very real sense to be with His disciples, and they with Him, among all nations until the end of the ages, and individually whenever two or more are gathered in His name. Christ's presence in the Church is undeniable. He is present in a real sense through His word and sacraments as the second person of the Godhead. Through the visible Church, He is at work.

---

[9] Acts 5:30-31
[10] John 15:26, 27
[11] Packer, p. 119
[12] *Book of Common Prayer*,1928. New York: The Church Hymnal Corporation, The Church Pension Fund, 1790, 1945; I John 2:1, 2

Christ's presence in His Church also is revealed in Her sacred ministry. Because of the relationship of the incarnate Word to the Father and the Holy Spirit, He is present in the Godhead and in His humanity whenever the Father and the Holy Spirit are present. The presence of Christ in the Sacraments is linked to His presence in the Church, to which the Sacraments have been entrusted, and in its sacred ministry, the Church is charged with the administration of the sacraments. Because the Church is the body of Christ, it is the particular vehicle of His presence in the world. It is often said that the Father uses the sacraments to draw us near to His Son.

> **The presence of Christ in the Sacraments is linked to His presence in the Church, to which the Sacraments have been entrusted, and in its sacred ministry, the Church is charged with the administration of the sacraments.**

Christ's Church is not a purely human institution speaking purely human words and performing purely human actions. Rather, Jesus Christ is at the center through His word and sacrament. The Church is engaged in passing on His word and administering His sacraments. God is acting through and in His visible Church. His sacred ministry is charged to proclaim His word and to administer His sacraments. It is worth noting that Christ does not merely empower His ordained representatives to act, but He acts through them. As the Head of the Church, He governs and sanctifies the Church through the Holy Spirit.[13]

**The Sacrament of Baptism**

> *Go therefore and make disciples, baptizing them*
> *in the name of the Father and of the Son and of the Holy Spirit.*
> *(Matthew 28:19)*

The true minister of Holy Baptism is our Lord and Savior. In the first of the sacraments instituted by Christ, His real presence is there, even

---

[13] Piepkorn, Arthur C. *Christ Today: His Presence in the Sacraments*. Originally published in *Lutheran World*, July 1963. http://pseudepigraph.us/wp-content/uploads/2014/05/Christ-Today-His-Presence-in-the-Sacraments.pdf, p. 3

though He makes use of human hands to pour and immerse and human lips to repeat the sacramental rite. It is through this sacrament that He brings us into the fellowship of His church. In his letter to the Ephesians, Paul talks of Christ's love for His Church in His act of giving Himself for her, "that He might sanctify and cleanse her with the washing of water by the word,"[14] thus making us holy. We become one in Christ Jesus through baptism, "For as many of you as have been baptized into Christ have put on Christ."[15] It is worth noting that being baptized in the name of God is to be baptized into the grace of God. God the Father is present, God the Son is present, and God the Holy Spirit is present in this action.[16] "Through baptism in the name of the Father and of the Son and of the Holy Spirit [the] commission of salvation becomes a vivid event that includes the sending of the Son and Holy Spirit. The 'Son' implements his salvific authority in Christian baptism."[17]

In explaining Paul's description of baptism given in his letter to the Romans 6:3-4,[18] Gruden notes that baptism is the symbolism of union with Christ in His death, burial, and resurrection.[19] This thought is elaborated in Paul's letter to the Colossians: "In Him . . . were buried with Him in baptism, in which you also were raised with *Him* through faith in the working of God, who raised Him from the dead."[20]

### The Sacrament of The Lord's Supper

*"...this do in remembrance of Me." (Luke 22:19)*
*"But I say to you, I will not drink of this fruit of the vine from now on until that day when I drink it new with you in My Father's kingdom." (Matthew 26: 29)*

Christ's presence also takes place in the Eucharistic bread and wine. In the Word of the gospel, Christ, the Word Incarnate, continues to speak to

---

[14] Ephesians 5:26, 27
[15] Galatians 3:27
[16] Piepkorn, p. 3
[17] Schnackenburg, Rudolph. *Jesus in the Gospels: A Biblical Christology.* Louisville, KY: Westminster John Knox Press, English translation, 1995, p. 99-100
[18] "O do you not know that as many of us as were baptized into Christ Jesus were baptized into His death? We were buried therefore with him by baptism into death? Therefore we were buried with Him through baptism into death, that just as Christ was raised from the dead by the glory of the Father, even so we also should walk in newness of life."
[19] Gruden, Wayne. *Systematic Theology: An Introduction to Biblical Doctrine.* Grand Rapids, MI: Zondervan Publishing House, 1994, p. 968
[20] Colossians 2:11, 12

us. In the sacrament of the table, He gives to us the same that He gave to the twelve at the Last Supper. We consecrate the giving of his true Body, which was sacrificed on the cross and raised from the dead three days later. This brings us to Him and Him to us in what we call a "remembrance" of that event that occurred more than two thousand years ago. Believers in Christ as the means of salvation submit to Him through baptism and move toward a living communion with Him through the celebration of the Eucharist.

The Jewish custom of the father of the house beginning a meal with the breaking of bread and its distribution coupled with a blessing foreshadows Jesus' action at the Last Supper. The bread that our Lord hands to His disciples is His body, which is given for the participants.[21] This gesture is a reference to the atoning death that Christ will bear for all of mankind. "Likewise He also *took* the cup after supper, saying 'This cup *is* the new covenant in My blood, which is shed for you."[22] This gesture is an even greater emphasis of the statement of His ultimate sacrifice for the sins of humanity. The "breaking of bread" continues as the resurrected Lord meets His disciples on the road. After explaining to them about Himself in the Scriptures, ". . . as He sat at the table with them, that He took bread, blessed and broke *it*, and gave it to them. Then their eyes were opened and they knew Him; and He vanished form their sight."[23]

> The Jewish custom of the father of the house beginning a meal with the breaking of bread and its distribution coupled with a blessing foreshadows Jesus' action at the Last Supper.

This practice continues today in the Church's breaking of bread. Christ is present for us in the celebration of the Eucharist in that He comes to us and He lays hold on us.[24] In the bread and wine, His body and blood has been offered and received by those who truly seek him.[25] In his book on Jesus and the Gospels, Schnackenburg explains that

---

[21] Luke 22:19
[22] Luke 22:20
[23] Luke 24:30-31
[24] Philippians 3:12
[25] Schnackenburg, p. 169

the linking of the understanding of the church with the death of Jesus, the Last Supper is instructive. Even if it is connected with difficult tradition-historical and exegetical problems, it is still certain that for the evangelists Jesus wanted to found a special celebrative meal that preserves the memory of his suffering and death and guarantees the participants in the meal a share in the body of Jesus and his "blood of the covenant" (Mark 14:22-25). Breaking through here is the view of the post-Easter church, which celebrates this feast and on its way into the perfected kingdom (14:25) constantly experiences through that meal the presence of the crucified Lord. The idea of the kingdom of God and its coming, which Jesus saw approaching in spite of his imminent departure, motivates the church in its view of the crucified and resurrected Jesus.[26]

There is no doubt that Christ works through His church and its ministers, but as Lutheran professor Arthur Piepkorn points out in an article published in 1963 issue of *Lutheran World*, Christ is also working through the Eucharistic participant. The celebration of the Eucharist is a sacrifice of praise and thanksgiving, a response to God's gift to us. Reception of Holy Communion "is a renewed challenge to, and a renewed act of, commitment to him. . . . and fortifies our union with him."[27] As Eucharistic participants, we receive the gifts of God so that they might strengthen us as individuals in faith toward God and that we might also increase our love for one another through Christ Jesus. When we offer ourselves to the service of God and to other members in the Body of Christ, it is Christ acting through us.

## Conclusion

As Christians, we make confession for human errors by acknowledging our manifold sins and wickedness. We ask for the Father to forgive our transgressions through Christ Jesus our Lord. Christ has already paid the price of sin by His death on the cross, but because of our human condition we stray from time to time. Christ is

---

[26] Schnackenburg, p. 43
[27] Piepkorn, p. 7

always present as we seek absolution for our sins. The absolution we receive is an effective means of imparting the grace of God. It is a way in which the presence of Christ working through the Holy Spirit, through His church, and through the ministry of the Church is made known. The penitent in the presence of Almighty God seeks to turn his life around, asking for remission of his sin. The work of Jesus Christ the God-man makes this action possible, and the sacraments give testimony to that fact.

# Chapter Two

# BOOK OF ACTS
## Transition from Gospels to Epistles

T he fifth book of the New Testament has been known from ancient times as "The Acts of the Apostles," a title that cannot be found in the book itself[28] and one that has been questioned:

> In almost all the editions of Scripture it is called "The Acts of the Apostles." But as you read the book through, the only ones whose acts are referred to are Peter and Paul. All the others are left almost entirely unnoticed, so the title is hardly fitting. It really should be titled, "The Acts of the Holy Spirit," or even perhaps, "The Continuing Acts of the Lord Jesus Christ" .... what the book of Acts is all about .... is the account of the way the Holy Spirit, coming into the church, continued what Jesus began to do, that is, carried on the work which was initiated during the days of his incarnation.[29]

The book covers a period of a little more than thirty years, tracing the origins of the early Church. The principle characters are Peter and Paul. There is little doubt that the book is the work of Luke, "the beloved physician," one of Paul's associates and a Gentile convert.

## A Bridge Between the Old and New Covenants

T he book of Acts reveals the power of the early Church. In doing so, it serves as an important bridge or transition from the narratives of the Gospels, which actually are part of the "old covenant," to the epistles, in which we have the "new covenant" teachings of Paul and

---

[28] White, Ellen G. *The Acts of the Apostles*. Christian Classics Ethereal Library, Calvin College. http://www.ccel.org/cel/white/acts.i.html

[29] Stedman,Ray C. The Acts of the Apostles: An Unfinished Story. http://www.pbc.org/dp/stedman/adventure/0245.html

other apostles. Hence, the book of Acts is vitally important to our understanding of how these two portions of Scripture are related and, in fact, some commentators have suggested that if Acts were removed from the "New Testament," we would never understand the rest of it.    Of this aspect, Bob Deffinbaugh notes that

> The Gospels end in Jerusalem with no church, a few Jewish believers in Jesus, and a group of disciples who are still living, as it were, in the past.  The Epistles, on the other hand, depict a growing number of churches made up of mainly Gentile believers and a group of disciples who are boldly proclaiming Christ as Israel's Messiah, and as the Savior of the Gentiles as well.  Only Acts fills in the gaps, to explain how these changes took place.  We would not understand  the Epistles apart from the Book of Acts.[30]

Ron Merryman makes a similar comment:

> . . . were *Acts* omitted from the canon, the New Testament would lose its historical continuity . . . . Think on this: What if there were no *Book of Acts* in the New Testament? What if upon completing John's Gospel, you were immediately confronted with the opening words of *Romans*, "Paul...an apostle...to all that be in Rome... (1:1,7)?" Questions that you could not answer would plague your mind. "Who is Paul?" "What is an Apostle?" "Who are these Believers in Rome"? "What is a 'church'?" No *Book of Acts* , no answer to these questions!
> *Acts* clearly serves as the historical bridge that takes us from the Gospels (and their unique message) to *Romans* and the Pauline letters (and Paul's unique message). [31]

Without the book of Acts, we would have little understanding of the power of the Holy Spirit, of His coming on the Day or Pentecost, or of the life-changing events that occurred as a result. We would have no

---

[30] Deffinbaugh, Bob.  Getting Ahead of God: The Importance of the Book of Acts.
    http://www.bible.org/page.asp?page_id=2123
[31] Merryman, Ron.  The Transitional Nature of Acts. Part I.
    http://www.duluthbible.org/g_f_j/TRANSITIONAL_NATURE_OF_ACTS.htm

record or understanding of how the Church was born nor how it grew in those early days. We also would have no knowledge of the background of how the apostle Paul, a persecutor of the Church, became its preeminent missionary; of how his apostleship was established; or of the connection between Jesus' teachings and those of the apostles. From the Book of Acts, we discover the gospel breaking from the confines of its Jewish origins and being transported from Jerusalem, the fortress of Judaism, to Rome, the center of Gentile culture, to the four corners of the Gentile world. For this reason,

**Without the book of Acts, we would have little understanding of the power of the Holy Spirit, of His coming on the Day or Pentecost, or of the life-changing events that occurred as a result.**

It is not insignificant that in the canonical order, Acts has been placed between the gospels and the epistles. It serves as a link between the records of Jesus and the apostolic correspondence. In many ways, the epistles are not fully intelligible until they are read against the backdrop of the book of Acts. The book shows effectively the main trends in the development of Christianity. It therefore makes a vital contribution to an understanding of the relationship between the teaching of Jesus and the apostolic doctrine.[32]

## Birth of the Church

We learn first of the coming of the Holy Spirit and the implications for salvation. Luke begins Acts the same way in which he concludes his Gospel, with the ascension of Jesus Christ into heaven.[33] It is from this point that we move forward to the Day of Pentecost, the day the Church was born. On that day, the disciples, having "fully come, they were all with one accord in one place."[34] Then, "suddenly there came a sound from heaven, as of a rushing mighty wind, and it filled the

---

[32] Anonymous. New Testament Study Helps: Acts of the Apostles.
http://www.theologywebsite.com/nt/acts.shtml
[33] Luke 24:51, Acts 1:1-9
[34] Acts 2:1

whole house where they were sitting. Then there appeared to them divided tongues, as of fire, and one sat upon each of them."[35]

Having received this Great Commission, and being empowered by the Holy Spirit, the disciples were ready to go forth to bear witness to the world of the saving grace of Christ Jesus.

Pentecost, by tradition, came fifty days after the offering of the first fruits and was also the celebration of the wheat harvest.[36] Later, Jews associated Pentecost with the giving of the Law on Sinai. The Pentecost event occurred as Christ had told them it would, having "commanded them not to depart from Jerusalem but to wait for the promise of the Father."[37] Jesus had instructed them while He was still with them that "John indeed baptized with water, but you shall be baptized with the Holy Spirit."[38]

At that time, they had asked the Lord if He would restore the kingdom to Israel, but Christ had told them it was not for them to know the Father's plan but that they would receive power when the Holy Spirit came upon them, and He had said to them, "you shall be witness to Me in Jerusalem, and in all Judea, and Samaria, and to the end of the earth."[39] Having received this Great Commission, and being empowered by the Holy Spirit, the disciples were ready to go forth to bear witness to the world of the saving grace of Christ Jesus.

### Early Christian Witness

The Church's early foundational work and preaching are chronicled in the book of Acts. The first to speak is Peter, who explains to the amazed crowd what has happened:

> "Men of Judea, and all who dwell at Jerusalem, let this be known to you, and heed my words: For these are not drunken, as you suppose, since it is *only* the third hour of

---

[35] Acts 2:2, 3
[36] Leviticus 23:10-21
[37] Acts 1:4
[38] Acts 11:16
[39] Acts 1:8

the day. But this is what was spoken by the prophet Joel: 'And it shall come to pass in the last days, sys God, That I will pour out of My Spirit on all flesh: Your sons and your daughters shall prophesy, Your young men shall see visions, Your old men shall dream dreams; . . . And it shall come to pass *That* whoever shall call on the name of the Lord Shall be saved."[40]

The Gospels tell a story of the *beginning* of Christ's work, which the book of Acts demonstrates is to continue through a totally new means. We find that the Holy Spirit, who merely came upon individuals in the Old Testament, now comes to fulfill the designed plan of God's work by filling the instrument that Christ has left behind, the Church. Stedman emphasizes the importance of the forming of a new people — the Church.

> Throughout the far-flung corners of the world, the Church continues the work today through the power of the Holy Spirit.

One hundred and twenty individuals met in the temple courts. They were as unrelated to each other as any people born in widely scattered parts of the earth might be to each other today. They were individually related to the Lord, but they had no blood ties. When the Holy Spirit was poured out on them, he baptized them into one body. They became a living unit; they were no longer related only to the Lord; they were related to each other. They became a living organism, which was from then on, and still is, the means by which he speaks to the world, by which he is given a flesh and blood existence tin our day.[41]

Throughout the far-flung corners of the world, the Church continues the work today through the power of the Holy Spirit. Clearly, as Peter explains, the Spirit of God initiates the change that is necessary for carrying out the work of God.

---

[40] Acts 2:14-21
[41] Stedman, Unfinished Story

An early instance of this power is recorded in Acts when Philip, one of the disciples, was preaching the Gospel in Samaria. The Spirit took hold and through an angel of the Lord commanded him to retreat from his preaching and go south into the desert to talk to one man:

> So he arose and went. And behold, a man of Ethiopia, a eunuch of great authority under Candace the queen of the Ethiopians, who had charge of all her treasury, and had come to Jerusalem to worship, was returning. And sitting in his chariot, he was reading Isaiah the prophet. Then the Spirit said to Philip, "Go near and overtake this chariot."
>
> So Philip ran to him, and heard him reading the prophet Isaiah, and said, "Do you understand what you are reading?" And he said, "How can I, unless someone guides me?" And he asked Philip to come up and sit with him. The place in the Scripture which he read was this:
> "He was led as a sheep to the slaughter;
> And as a lamb before its shearer *is* silent,
> So He opened not His mouth.
> In His humiliation His justice was taken away,
> And who will declare His generation?
> For His life is taken from the earth."
> So the eunuch answered Philip and said, "I ask you, of whom does the prophet say this, of himself or of some other man?"
>
> Then Philip opened his mouth, and beginning at this Scripture, preached Jesus to him. Now as they went down the road, they came to some water. And the eunuch said, "See, *here is* water. What hinders me from being baptized?"
>
> Then Philip said, "If you believe with all your heart, you may."
>
> And he answered and said, "I believe that Jesus Christ is the Son of God."
>
> So he commanded the chariot to stand still. And both Philip and the eunuch went down into the water, and he baptized him.[42]

---

[42] Acts 8:27-38

In this account, we discover the power of the "Spirit-led witnessing . . . the right man in the right place at the right time saying the right thing to the right person." This is one of the first examples of the power of the directing activity of the Holy Spirit.[43]

The Church, being empowered by the Holy Spirit, is the Body whose task it is to help lead men to salvation. Through His Church, Christ reveals His fullness and His sufficiency. The members of his Church are those whom he has called out of darkness into his light to show forth His glory. God intends that "his manifold wisdom . . . might be made known by the church to the principalities and powers in the heavenly *places*, according to the eternal purpose which He accomplished in Christ Jesus, our Lord, in whom we have boldness and access with confidence through faith in Him."[44] In the book of Isaiah, we find the promises regarding the Church: "Mine house shall be called a house of prayer for all people."[45] We also are told in Ezekiel that

> "I will make them and the places round all around My hill a blessing; and I will cause showers to come down in their season; there shall be showers of blessing. . . . .And I will raise up for them a garden for renown, and they shall no longer be consumed with hunger in the land, nor bear the shame of the Gentiles anymore. Thus they shall know that I, the Lord their God *am* with them, and they, the house of Israel, *are* My people," the Lord God. "You are MY flock, the flock of My pasture; you *are* men, *and* I *am* your God," says the Lord God.[46]

## The Primary Focus: the Resurrection

The book of Acts focuses on the power of the resurrected Christ working in His Church through the Holy Spirit. The concept of resurrection was not articulated very strongly in the Old Testament until the Book of Daniel, speaking of the righteous and the unrighteous:

---

[43] Stedman, 1955, p. 23
[44] Ephesians 3:10-12
[45] Isaiah 56:7
[46] Ezekiel 34:26, 29-31

"At that time Michael shall stand up,
The great prince who stands *watch* over the sons of your
people;
And there shall be a time of trouble,
Such as never was since there was a nation,
*Even* to that time.
And at that time your people shall be delivered,
Every one who is found written in the book.
And many of those who sleep in the dust of the earth shall
awake,
Some to everlasting life,
Some to shame *and* everlasting contempt."[47]

**For the early Church, the Resurrection of Christ was of great significance. It was the cornerstone of their preaching.**

Daniel B. Wallace addresses this question: Why was it not clearly revealed until then? One reason he offers as to why it was not revealed was that it was not necessary to reveal it at that time. While the Jews were in captivity, they had no hope for the present; they could only look to the future. The revelation of the resurrection and the life to come came at precisely the right time when people needed hope for the future.[48]

For the early Church, the Resurrection of Christ was of great significance. It was the cornerstone of their preaching. In his sermon explaining the coming of the Holy Spirit, Peter explains the importance of the Resurrection, which is at the center of his sermon:

"Men of Israel, hear these words: Jesus of Nazareth, a Man attested by God to you by miracles, wonders, and signs which God did through Him in your midst, as you yourselves also know—Him, being delivered by the determined purpose and foreknowledge of God, you have taken by lawless hands, have crucified, and put to death; whom God raised up, having loosed the pains of

---

[47] Daniel 12:1,2
[48] Wallace, Daniel B. Acts: Introduction, Outline, and Argument.
http://www.bible.org/docs/soapbox/actsotl.htm

death, because it was not possible that He should be held by it."[49]

We can examine and realize how important it was by looking at several other passages in the book of Acts. After Judas' death, it was necessary to select another apostle, and in doing so, the disciples determined that "beginning from the baptism of John to that

**Because of Christ's Resurrection, we, too, will be raised.**

day when He was taken up from us, one of these must become a witness with us of His resurrection."[50] We learn from this passage not only the importance of the resurrection to the disciples but also its importance with regard to *being* one of the apostles. Without the book of Acts, we would not have this information, nor would we understand why Paul often makes an issue of "being an apostle" in his letters (as he was not a witness to the resurrection).

In another sermon, Peter once again focuses on the resurrection when he tells the Jews that they "killed the Prince of life; whom God raised from the dead; whereof we are witnesses."[51] In Acts 4:8, we find the power of the Holy Sprit pouring out of Peter as he preaches the resurrected Christ. The resurrection is especially important, too, with regard to the "blessing" God promised Abraham:

> The root of the blessedness is the resurrection of the dead . . . . It is the fact that the resurrection of the dead is the root of blessedness promised which gives to the interrogation [of Paul before King Agrippa] its point . . . . The blessedness promised is the removal of the curse which is resting upon man and his entire environment, and that curse cannot be removed without his resurrection from the dead. Resurrection is a re-standing or standing again, not in some stage of a fallen or based state or condition, but in Adam's original state and condition, which was in every respect "very good."[52]

---

[49] Acts 2:22-24
[50] Acts 1:22
[51] Acts 3:15
[52] Anonymous. "One Hope." http://www.divineplan.org/htdbv5/r1434b.htm

Because of Christ's Resurrection, we, too, will be raised.

## Redeeming Grace: Salvation of a Persecutor

Another critically important aspect of Acts, the account of how a persecutor of the Church became its foremost missionary of all times, is found in the ninth chapter of the Book of Acts, where we learn of a man on the road to Damascus who encounters the power of the Holy Spirit – a man who until that moment zealously persecuted members of the Way.

The first "snapshot" we have of him occurs earlier, when we read of the first persecution and martyrdom—the stoning of Stephen.  After preaching a long sermon in which he related the history of Israel and its failure to listen to the prophets sent by God, Stephen called the Jews of his day "stiffnecked and uncircumcised in heart and ears." He then asked them if they "do always resist the Holy Ghost: as [their]fathers did,"[53] to which the multitudes "cried out with a loud voice, stopped their ears, and ran at him with one accord;  and they cast *him* out of the city and stoned *him*. And the witnesses laid down their clothes at the feet of a young man named Saul."[54]

That same young man, with misguided godly intentions, later took up a cause to persecute the Church, but that was about to change. We read that as he journeyed,

> he came near Damascus, and suddenly a light shone
> around him from heaven. 4 Then he fell to the ground, and
> heard a voice saying to him, "Saul, Saul, why are you
> persecuting Me?"
> And he said, "Who are You, Lord?"
> Then the Lord said, "I am Jesus, whom you are
> persecuting. It *is* hard for you to kick against the goads."
> So he, trembling and astonished, said, "Lord, what do You
> want me to do?"
> Then the Lord *said* to him, "Arise and go into the city, and
> you will be told what you must do."[55]

---

[53] Acts 7:51
[54] Acts 7:57-58
[55] Acts 9:3-6

The Spirit sent another man to pray with Saul; this man, Ananias, did not understand his call but became an instrument in this Spirit-filled work. Saul, known to us as Paul, became a truly great apostle of Christ. Blinded by his encounter with the Savior of the world, his eyes were opened to a new light, the Light of the World!

Throughout the centuries, the Church has faced darkness, conflict, and persecution. As noted, Paul himself was actively engaged in the persecution before his conversion and was the victim of it many times afterwards. Never has a dark cloud fallen on God's Church that He has not foreseen, is not prepared for, nor has planned to counter, but we need Acts to understand the history and nature of the opposition to the Gospel. Again, Deffinbaugh provides an interesting commentary on this matter:

> Never has a dark cloud fallen on God's Church that He has not foreseen, is not prepared for, nor has planned to counter, but we need Acts to understand the history and nature of the opposition to the Gospel.

One of the greatest and most frequent problems the New Testament church had to deal with was the opposition of the Jews, who resisted the gospel, and the Judaizers, who sought to pervert it. The Gospel of Luke (and the other Gospels as well) describe the roots of this opposition, which began as a resistance to Jesus' actions and teaching. The book of Acts shows how this opposition continued on against the gospel and the church after the death, burial, and resurrection of our Lord. What Paul does theologically in the Book of Romans, Luke does historically in the Book of Acts. We would never understand the nature of the problem which faced the church (which, incidentally, has its own forms today) apart from Luke/Acts.[56]

Wonderful is the work that God has designed to accomplish through His Church, to the glory of His name. God's chosen people, the people of

---

[56] Deffinbaugh

Israel, were the ones that He had selected to reveal His character. The people of Israel lost sight of their high station and privileges as God's representatives. Many of them had lost sight of their holy mission by forgetting their duty to God. They imposed greater restrictions on themselves than God had placed upon them in terms of the association with other people, thus creating a wall of separation between themselves and other nations. Ellen White states that "the Jewish people robbed God of the service He required of them, and they robbed their fellowmen of religious guidance and holy example."[57]

The people of Israel were content to follow their path of legalism and ceremonialism –"the faith that works by love and purifies the soul could find no place in the religion of the Pharisees."[58] In Jeremiah, God had declared that He "had planted [them] a noble vine, a seed of the highest quality. How then have you turned before Me?"[59] Israel was meant to take God's message to others, but instead "Israel [emptied] his vine, and [brought] forth fruit for himself."[60] In Isaiah 5:3-6, we learn that the Lord will, like a farmer whose efforts have been fruitless, take away the protection that he has afforded his people. The Jewish leaders considered themselves too wise to need instruction, too righteous to need salvation, too highly honored to need the honor that comes from Christ. So, "it was not through the obedience of Israel that the Gentiles received the gospel but actually through their disobedience. . . . [Acts] is an account of the sovereignty and power of God, using even men's sin to accomplish His purposes."[61]

> So, the message of salvation turned from the Jews to the rest of the world. And Paul was called to take that message to the Gentiles.

So, the message of salvation turned from the Jews to the rest of the world. And Paul was called to take that message to the Gentiles.

---

[57] White
[58] Ibid.
[59] Jeremiah 2:21
[60] Hosea 10:1
[61] Deffinbaugh

**36**

## Paul: Missionary to the Gentiles

The book of Acts also relates the events in Paul's life after his conversion experience, and then Luke provides the narrative of Paul's missionary endeavors, particularly his three missionary journeys, his trials and appeal to Rome, and his time in Rome. In each town along the way, Paul started out in the synagogues, but the Lord had said to Ananias when he sent him to get Paul that the latter was "a chosen vessel of Mine to bear My name before Gentiles, kings, and the children of Israel."[62] Finally, while with Barnabas in Antioch in Pisidia, where the Jews had rejected the message, Paul announced that

> "It was necessary that the word of God should be spoken to you first; but since you reject it, and judge yourselves unworthy of everlasting life, behold, we turn to the Gentiles. For so the Lord has commanded us: 'I have set you as a light to the Gentiles, that you should be for salvation to the ends of the earth.'"[63]

In this event, we see recorded in Acts the beginning of the far-reaching efforts of the early church as it moved from a Jerusalem-centered movement to a universal Christ-centered movement spreading to the entire world. The Book of Acts provides us with an inspired account of this transition. The Gospel no longer has a purely Jewish context but takes on a more universal one that embraces the Gentiles, becoming a mostly Gentile phenomenon. This transition has two major facets: the coming of the Holy Spirit upon Gentile believers[64] and the decision of the Jerusalem council with regard to circumcision, namely that the Gentiles did not need to be circumcised, their salvation being testimony to that fact.[65]

## Paul's Imprisonment and the Furtherance of the Gospel

Acts begins in Jerusalem with a handful of Jewish followers of our Lord and ends in Rome with a number of Gentile churches having been founded in mostly Gentile communities along the way. As already

---

[62] Acts 9:15
[63] Acts 13:46, 47
[64] Acts 15:8, 9
[65] Acts 15:12-35

alluded to, the Church moved from its geographical roots and at the same time moved theologically away from Israel. Hence, we see again the importance of Acts, for it explains the origins of the churches to whom the epistles were written. With the account provided by Luke, "we know much about the church and how it started . . . [we have] valuable background information for the churches that are addressed in the Epistles."[66]

We not only have the account of the Gospel breaking forth from the confines of its Jewish origins and being transported from Jerusalem, the fortress of Judaism, to other areas, but in the latter part, we also learn how it made its way to Rome, the center of Gentile culture, and we are conscious of Paul's defense of the Gospel and his calling. He makes several important appearances after being arrested, and in each one of them, he seizes the opportunity to preach the Gospel while giving an account of his ministry.

Despite being forewarned of impending danger in Jerusalem, Paul proceeded to the city and went to the temple, where he was accused of profaning the temple and also of being the Egyptian false prophet who was a leader of a rebellion.

After being beaten by the crowd, Paul was rescued by Roman guards and led away to military barracks to be protected from the Jewish mob. In the safety of the garrison, he proclaimed in his defense that he was "a Jew from Tarsus, in Cilicia, a citizen of no mean city."[67] We find him going through a series of trials that Luke records in great detail, perhaps to be used as a defense for Paul, who first appeared before the Sanhedrin. They were outraged at his statements, and a plot was formed to kill him, but instead of being detrimental to Paul, it actually resulted in his gaining more protection from the Romans. Under their protection, he was taken to Caesarea to be tried before Felix, the Roman governor. For a period of two years, Paul was submitted to various trials, first before Felix, then Festus, and then Agrippa II. When questioned by Felix about returning to Jerusalem to be tried before the Jews for the charges they brought against, Paul refused, appealing to Caesar:

---

[66] Deffinbaugh
[67] Acts 21:39

**38**

I stand at Caesar's judgment seat, where I ought to be judged. To the Jews I have done no wrong, as you very well know. For if I am an offender, or have committed anything deserving of death, I do not object to dying; but if there nothing in these things of which men accuse me, no one can deliver me to them. I appeal to Caesar.[68]

Festus' response was that "unto Caesar you shall go."[69] What is ironic is that Paul would have been found innocent, but because of his appeal, which he may have made because "he believed he would get fairer treatment from the Roman government than from his fellow countrymen,"[70] he was sent to Rome. Some people have suggested that Paul made a mistake, but the sovereignty of God was manifest in the fruit that came as a result of Paul's imprisonment.

The book of Acts ends with Paul in prison, chained to a guard, but it is not a negative ending. Although Paul was limited and bound, the Gospel was not. In fact, Stedman notes several positive results that came from Paul's imprisonment, one of which was that the other brethren in the city were busy preaching the Gospel, "so there was more of the gospel going out in Rome because he was in prison than there would have been if he were loose,"[71] and Paul greatly rejoiced in that fact. Furthermore, the imprisonment served in other ways to advance the Gospel, for

> The cream of the crop in the Roman army who formed the special palace guard of the emperor were being brought to Christ one by one. The praetorium guard was being reached, and, of course, you know how it was happening. They were being brought in by the emperor's command

---

[68] Acts 25:10-11
[69] Acts 25:12
[70] Wallace
[71] Stedman

and chained to the Apostle Paul for six hours. Talk about a captive audience![72]

Perhaps one of the greatest advantages to Paul's imprisonment are the prison letters we have today, which might never have been written otherwise. Paul's time in prison allowed him the opportunity to write holy Scripture that has been used of the Holy Spirit, about whom Acts really focuses, to convert Jews and Gentiles alike for almost 2,000 years. And so Acts ends with Paul imprisoned, but with the testimony that no one and nothing can imprison the Gospel. It also is a record of the testimony given by Paul in his letter to the Romans concerning God's sovereignty:

> *". . . all things work together for good to those who love God, to those who are the called according to His purpose."*[73]

---

[72] Ibid.
[73] Romans 8:28

## Chapter Three

# THE BIBLICAL COVENANT
## A Glimpse of Covenant in Nuptial Terms

The Bible is the inspired Word of God, the book that chronicles God's irrevocable bond with His creation. It is the story of humanity's origins, fall, salvation, and eventual glorification through the saving work of the Lord Christ Jesus. Contained within it are numerous covenants, and an important approach to understanding the unfolding story of God's redemption in Scripture is the study of the covenants, or Covenant Theology.

Why is the study of the covenants so important? Numerous answers can be given, including the fact that the study of Covenant Theology is crucial to grasping a thorough understanding of God's redemptive work. It is important because, biblically and theologically speaking, it provides the bridge between anthropology and soteriology. The study of covenants gives us a greater understanding of the relationship that God has with his creation. Further, the entire structure of the Bible is covenantal in nature. Michael Horton notes that the covenant forms

> that particular architectural structure that we believe the Scriptures themselves to yield . . . . it is not simply the concept of the covenant, but the concrete existence of God's covenantal dealings in our history that provides the context within which we recognize the unity of Scripture amid it [sic] remarkable variety.[74]

Steven Baugh, writing in *Modern Reformation.*[75] says that "Covenant Theology is not incidental to Reformed Theology – It is reformed theology."

---

[74] Horton, Michael S. *God of Promise: Introducing Covenant Theology.* Grand Rapids, MI: Baker, Quoted in Gentry and Wellum, p. 57

[75] Baugh, Steven M. "Covenant Theology Illustrated: Romans 5 on the Federal Headship of Adam and Christ." *Modern Reformation* July/August 9 (4), 2000, pp. 16-23

The term *covenant* is also used to illustrate the breadth and scope in the redemptive history of God's people. The Psalms mention God's covenant with David in the Old Testament (e.g., Ps 89:1-4). In the New Testament, the writer to the Hebrews tell us that Christ is the mediator of the New Covenant (Hebrews 12:24), instituted during the last Passover He shared with His disciples:

> And as they were eating, Jesus took bread, blessed and broke *it*, and gave *it* to the disciples and said, "Take, eat; this is My body." Then He took the cup, and gave thanks, and gave *it* to them, saying, "Drink from it, all of you. For this is My blood of the new covenant, which is shed for many for the remission of sins. But I say to you, I will not drink of this fruit of the vine from now on until that day when I drink it new with you in My Father's kingdom."[76]

For these and many other reasons, it behooves us to undertake a study of Biblical covenants.

In this chapter, I will summarize some of the main considerations of covenants and then will look at how a long-neglected approach, that of covenant in nuptial terms, provides additional insights into God's dealings with humanity.

## Definitions and Purposes of Covenants

In English, the word *covenant* signifies a mutual understanding between two or more parties, each bound to fulfill specific obligations. It is a legal agreement, usually written. It is a solemn agreement to do or not to do certain things. In the Bible, covenants take on more profound implications. A covenant is defined as a "bond in blood sovereignly administered." A covenant is a life-and-death matter. A covenant is sacrosanct.[77] The term *berit* in Hebrew is used to define a compact that is made by passing through flesh. Thus, we find the expression: "cutting a covenant" or "covenant cutting." In Genesis, we find an example of this use:

---

[76] Matthew 26:26-29
[77] Robertson, O. Palmer. *The Christ of the Covenants*. Phillipsburg, NJ: Presbyterian and Reformed Publishing Co., 1980, p. 4

And it came to pass, when the sun went down and it was dark, that behold, there appeared a smoking oven and a burning torch that passed between those pieces. On the day *the Lord made a covenant with Abram,* saying, "To your descendants I have given this land, from the river of Egypt to the great river, the River Euphrates, [the land of the] Kenites, the Kenizzites, the Kadmonites, the Hittites, the Perizzites, the Rephaim, the Amorites, the Canaanites, the Girgashites and the Jebusites.[78]

Another question that arises is: Why are covenants made? The answer is complex, but a basic understanding is that the intended purpose of the covenant is to bind two parties to a commitment, an interpersonal relationship. The entering into a covenantal bond binds or obligates the individuals in that relationship. For instance, Joshua was in covenant with the Gibeonites (Joshua 9:1-27) and Zedekiah made a covenant with Nebuchadnezzar (Jeremiah 34:8-18). Entering into a covenant also provides a strong sense of security. A good example of this is the marriage covenant, instituted by God to be a model for all covenants.[79]

> Divine covenants are an expression of God's will and His purpose for humanity. They are the means by which His will and purpose are fulfilled.

Divine covenants are an expression of God's will and His purpose for humanity. They are the means by which His will and purpose are fulfilled. Creation and redemption illustrate God's purpose for man.

---

[78] Genesis 15:17-21, emphasis mine.
[79] Conner, K and Ken Malmin. *The Covenants.* Portland, OR: City Bible Publishing, 1997, p. 6

## Aspects of Covenants

Almost all covenants were ratified by oath. When an oath was taken, the covenant became irrevocable (Matthew 14:9; Genesis 26:23, 33; Jeremiah 11:5). Oaths and promises bound the one who uttered it to fulfillment (Numbers 30:2, 10; 1 Samuel 14:26 - 28; II Chronicles 6:22; 15:15). Failure to take an oath as a condition of the covenant could result in changes and cancellations. The breaking of an oath resulted in certain consequences and brought a curse upon the one who broke it (Nehemiah 5:12; Zachariah 8:17; Matthew 14:9; Genesis 26:23, 33),[80] and "nothing less than the shedding of blood [could] relieve the obligations incurred in the event of covenantal violation."[81] In certain circumstances, a person in authority could release somebody from an oath (Genesis 24:8, 41).

All divine covenants contain parts or elements that can be summarized as words or promises, blood, and seal of the covenant. It is expressed as a bond, a bond-in-blood, and a bond-in-blood sovereignly administered.[82] The words of the covenant initiated by God contain the promises of blessings for fulfillment and the curses for failure to perform. There are natural, national, and temporal promises as well as spiritual promises. In divine covenants, these elements become irrevocable.[83]

The Edenic covenant or the "Covenant of Works" specifically spelled out to Adam, the first man, his obligation to his Creator:

> Then the Lord God took the man and put him in the garden of Eden to tend it and keep it. And the Lord God commanded the man, saying, "Of every tree of the garden may freely eat; but of the tree of the knowledge of good and evil you shall not eat, for in the day that you eat of it you shall surely die.[84]

Adam's failure to fulfill the terms of the covenant, by eating of the tree of the knowledge of good and evil, resulted in severe consequences, not just for him and the woman but for the entire human race (Romans 5:12).

---

[80] Ibid.
[81] Robertson, p. 11
[82] Ibid., p. 15
[83] Ibid., p. 7
[84] Genesis 2:15-17

After the fall, there followed a series of covenants that God made with successive generations. These covenants are the Adamic, Noahic, Abrahamic, Mosaic, Davidic, and New Covenants.

Covenants were considered a life-and-death commitment and were ratified with bloodshed. Covenantal sacrifices required a mediator and a high priest. Sacrificial action could occur only in a holy place such as an altar in the tabernacle or temple and required the presence of a priest. The sacrificial blood, which was used in the ratification process, represented the life commitment of those who entered into the covenant. Covenantal sacrifices involved both the shedding of blood and the death of the body. The solemnity of this act required both elements be present.[85]

The seal of the covenant was a valid witness to attest to the veracity of the covenant. It served as a constant reminder of the covenantal promise, its terms, and the authenticity of the covenant. All of the divine covenants had such a seal. They're referred to as *the seal of the covenant*, the *sign of the covenant*, or the *token of the covenant*. Frequently, the parties also engaged in a meal, which we see in many of the covenants God made, and in those between men. Regarding the latter, Dumbrell points out that the trust involved was expressed in a meal in the two covenants made between Abraham with Abimelech and Laban with Jacob.[86] The most notable was that of the New Covenant, which as noted above, Jesus Christ instituted on the night of the Passover meal with His disciples.

These covenants often also were accompanied by signs or pledges. For instance, in Genesis 9:9-17, God said to Noah and his sons with him, "I establish my covenant with you and your offspring after you . . . . that never again shall all flesh be cut off by the waters of the flood, and never

---

[85] Conner and Malmin, p. 7

[86] Dumbrell, William J. *Covenant and Creation: A Theology of Old Testament Covenants*. Eugene, OR: Wipf & Stock Publishers, 1984, pp. 17-18

again shall there be a flood to destroy the earth." Then, He gave a sign, saying, "This is the sign of the covenant that I make between me and you and every living creature that is with you . . . I have set my bow in the cloud, and it shall be a sign of the covenant between me and the earth." Various other covenants also have appropriate signs or symbols linked to them: Circumcision was the sign of the covenant with Abraham, and the Sabbath was a sign of the covenant with Israel at Mount Sinai.[87] Bishop Ray R. Sutton notes that

> The covenant with Abraham was cut by means of severed animals and fire. The fire indicated judgment sanction. Then, Abraham's personal reception was the rite of circumcision. Of course, circumcision was a "bloody" ordeal that also denotes cursing sanction in symbolic form. In the New Covenant, the symbols of the sanctions become baptism and communion . . . . The Lord's Supper is a visual manifestation of the finished work of Christ, which mediates life and death. It communicates life and death. If partaken wrongly, it kills the recipient (I Cor. 11:27-34).[88]

Sutton has demonstrated other aspects of covenants, based on Suzerain treaties, that tie all of these and other elements together. His book, *That You May Prosper*, is devoted to showing how all the covenants have these distinct elements:

• *Transcendence*, in the Biblical sense meaning that "there is a fundamental distinction between the Creator's Being and the creatures being." At the same time, "He is also present (immanent) with us. This presence of God is equally an aspect of true transcendence. No other being is fully transcendent, so no other being is universally present. God alone is omnipresent."[89]

• *Hierarchy*, in Biblical terms meaning a "series of courts with delegated authorities over each level. The procedure is from the bottom up." It has to do with God's authority, and "he makes His Lordship visible by

---

[87] Alexander, T. Desmond. Genesis Study Notes. *English Standard Version* (ESV). Wheaton, IL: Crossway Bibles Study Bible, Note on Genesis 9:12-17, page 65

[88] Sutton, Ray R. *That You May Prosper*. Tyler, TX: Institute for Christian Economics, 1992, 1997, pp. 86-87

[89] Sutton, *Prosper*, pp. 24-25

establishing representatives, a hierarchy. He establishes delegated authorities, who work from the bottom up, not a bureaucracy, working from the top down."[90]

• *Ethics*, which is based on God's establishing an *"ethical relationship between cause and effect* . . . . God dictates the terms . . . under which man can have a relationship with Him. . . . Man is called to be faithful to God by submitting to them."[91] This is the portion that deals with exclusive fidelity.

• *(Oath) Sanctions*, which are both the blessings and the curses that accompany the covenant. Sutton notes four aspects: they have to do with reception of inheritance, they are actually promises, they are judicial involving a judgment before blessing, and the sanctions are dual (blessing and cursing), both of which, rather than just one, are applied.[92]

• *(Sustainability)* Continuity, or the confirmation of a legitimate heir, thereby transferring inheritance to him; it is a process of confirmation.[93] –

A useful acronym for remembering them is **THEOS.**

## Types of Covenants

Peter Gentry and Stephen Wellum note that "the same word is used in Scripture for a wide diversity of oath-bound commitments in various relationships." They provide several different types of oaths found in the Old Testament, along with examples:

• international treaties – the treaty made by the Gibeonites with the Canaanites when Joshua led Israel into Canaan (Joshua 9)
• clan/tribal alliances – the agreement made in Genesis 14:13 was "essentially an alliance between clans or tribes.
• personal agreements – the agreement made between Laban and Jacob not to harm each other (Genesis 31:44)

---

[90] Ibid., p. 42
[91] Ibid., p. 60
[92] Ibid., pp. 78-79
[93] Ibid., pp. 103, 105

- *loyalty agreements* – the friendship agreement made between David and Jonathan, solemnized twice (I Samual 18:3; 23:18)

- marriage – a "loyalty agreement formally solemnized by a vow before God" (Proverbs 2:17; Malachi 2:14)

- natonal legal agreements – covenant between a king and  his people, such as King Zedekiah with his people to proclaim freedom for all the slaves (Jeremiah 34:8-10).[94]

## Parties Involved in Covenants

The Bible is replete with examples of covenants made between God and man, as well as covenants made between men. The former covenants are all unilateral in nature, initiated by God to man.

In the area of covenants between men, we find treaties, alliances, and leagues (e.g., Genesis 14:13; Exodus 23: 32, 34:12, 15; Joshua 9:6 –16).  We see examples of ordinances between monarchs and subjects in II Samuel 3:12, 13 and 5:3, and in Jeremiah 34:8-18. We also find agreements and pledges in II Kings 11:4 and Hosea 10:4. We observe alliances of friendship in I Samuel 18:3, as well as alliances of marriage in Proverbs 2:17 and Malachi 2:14. Men frequently made covenants with other men in relation to various matters, an example of which is the covenant made between Abraham and Abimelech concerning the well of Beersheba (Genesis 21:27, 31- 32).

In Scripture, when a covenant is instituted between God and man, God always is the initiator, for He alone has the mind, the authority, and the ability to make them effective. Man does not come to God with a proposal seeking God's approval; rather, it is God who comes to man declaring His authority and will and seeking the adherence of man. A common component is, "I will be your God, and you will be My people."

> In Scripture, when a covenant is instituted between God and man, God always is the initiator, for He alone has the mind, the authority, and the ability to make them effective.

---

[94] Gentry, Peter J. and Stephen J. Wellum. *Kingdom through Covenant: A Biblical-Theological Understanding of the Covenants.*  Wheaton, ILL: Crossway, 2012, pp. 130-131

The words of the covenant initiated by God contain the promises of blessings for fulfillment and the curses for failure to perform. There are natural, national, and temporal promises as well as spiritual promises. The terms are also spelled out that bind the grantor and the grantee. Finally, there is the oath which confirms the covenant. In a divine covenant, these elements become irrevocable.[95]

All covenants made by God are manifestations of God's grace, mercy, and love for his creation, but He does not force them on man or coerce him. Man has the choice of accepting or rejecting God's offer—but he cannot change it.

Man cannot be in a covenantal relationship with God until God chooses to reveal that covenant to man by openly declaring the promises and the terms. "The friendship of the LORD is for those who fear him, and he makes known to them his covenant"[96]; "And he declared to you his covenant, which he commanded you to perform, that is, the Ten Commandments, and he wrote them on two tablets of stone."[97]

> All covenants made by God are manifestations of God's grace, mercy, and love for his creation, but He does not force them on man or coerce him.

Man has proven that he is unable to fulfill his part of any covenant initiated by God. Hence, God also enables man to fulfill his part of the covenant. It is through the grace of God that man is able to make any nominal effort toward fulfillment. We see an illustration of this reality in Ephesians:

> But God, who is rich in mercy, because of His great love with which He loved us, even when we were dead in trespasses, made us alive together with Christ (by grace you have been saved), and raised *us* up together, and made *us* sit together in the heavenly *places* in Christ Jesus, that in the ages to come He might show the exceeding riches of His grace in *His* kindness toward us in Christ

---

[95] Robertson, p. 7
[96] Psalm 25:14
[97] Deuteronomy 4:13

Jesus. For by grace you have been saved through faith, and that not of yourselves; *it is* the gift of God, not of works, lest anyone should boast. For we are His workmanship, created in Christ Jesus for good works, which God prepared beforehand that we should walk in them. Therefore remember that you, once Gentiles in the flesh — who are called Uncircumcision by what is called the Circumcision made in the flesh by hands — that at that time you were without Christ, being aliens from the commonwealth of Israel and strangers from the covenants of promise, having no hope and without God in the world. But now in Christ Jesus you who once were far off have been brought near by the blood of Christ. For He Himself is our peace, who has made both one, and has broken down the middle wall of separation.[98]

God, on the other hand, is not only the Covenant *Maker* – He also is the Covenant *Keeper*. God does not forget or neglect the covenants that he makes; rather, he always follows through (Deuteronomy 7:9; II Chronicles 6:14; Psalm 111:5, 9; Romans 1:31). This confidence in God was pronounced by Peter on the Day of Pentecost when he preached his sermon, quoting from Psalm 16 and then explaining its meaning:

"Men *and* brethren, let *me* speak freely to you of the patriarch David, that he is both dead and buried, and his tomb is with us to this day. Therefore, being a prophet, and knowing that God had sworn with an oath to him that of the fruit of his body, according to the flesh, He would raise up the Christ to sit on his throne, he, foreseeing this, spoke concerning the resurrection of the Christ, that His soul was not left in Hades, nor did His flesh see corruption. This Jesus God has raised up, of which we are all witnesses. Therefore being exalted to the right hand of God, and having received from the Father the promise of the Holy Spirit, He poured out this which you now see and hear."[99]

---

[98] Ephesians 2:4-14
[99] Acts 2:29-33

## Emphases of Covenants

Scholars differ on what constitutes a covenant or what aspect of it should be emphasized. Among the different types of covenants or emphases, with a comment on each, are:

• "to cut" – As already noted, Robertson discusses covenants in terms of a bond, a bond-in-blood, and a bond-in-blood sovereignly administered. This approach emphasizes the death and shedding of blood that occurs with the covenants. He notes that this term is used repeatedly in Scripture.[100] It is seen in Eden, when God made coverings of skin for the man and the woman (Genesis 3), and then throughout Scripture until Jesus Christ sheds His blood on Calvary to redeem humanity. It is also seen many times in Revelation, with particular relevance toward the end:

> Now I saw heaven opened, and behold, a white horse!
> And He who sat on him *was* called Faithful and True, and
> in righteousness He judges and makes war. His eyes *were*
> like a flame of fire, and on His head *were* many crowns. He
> had a name written that no one knew except Himself. *He*
> *was clothed with a robe dipped in blood*, and His name is
> called is The Word of God.[101]

• "kinship" – Another approach focuses on the family and kinship, with emphases on the father, but notes how two parties engage in a mutual commitment with divine sanctions. Scott Hahn has developed this emphasis in his book, *Kinship by Covenant*. [102]

• juridical – This approach is based on the view of God's relationship in the Deuteronomic covenant as having legal components or aspects, and was put forth by Julius Wellhausen[103] and George Mendenhall.[104]

---

[100] Robertson, p. 11
[101] Revelation 19:11-13, emphasis mine.
[102] Hahn, Scott W. *Kinship by Covenant: A Canonical Approach to the Fulfillment of God's Saving Promises*. New Haven & London: Yale University Press, 2009
[103] According to Hahn.
[104] Mendenhall, G. E. *Law and Covenant in Israel and the Ancient Near East*. Pittsburgh, PA: Biblical Colloquium, 1955; Also according to Hahn, p. 2, footnote 5

• meal – As noted above, the meal plays an important part in the making of a covenant. Sutton notes that it is part of the aspect in which two become one, via another, without ceasing to be two.[105]

• relational – In addition to Hahn's argument for "kinship" is the emphasis on God's desire to enter into relationship with humanity, which Engelsma describes as one involving mutual love; this element relates to the exclusive fidelity that Sutton discusses in his course on Covenant Theology.

• nuptial – another emphasis, which has not been well-developed but has been presented by Adler is covenant as nuptial agreement.

## Covenant in Nuptial Terms

God's covenants contain not only the different aspects noted above but also an element that has not been adequately elucidated, the fact that they also are nuptial agreements. In addition to having nuptial emphases in the covenants themselves, the language of Scripture is replete with nuptial language, and, indeed, God uses nuptial language to describe His covenant with Israel, both in entering into relationship with her and in her violation of their "marriage." Nuptial language is used also in the New Testament to describe the relationship between Jesus Christ and His redeemed people, the Church.

> Nuptial language is used also in the New Testament to describe the relationship between Jesus Christ and His redeemed people, the Church.

Through His prophet Ezekiel, God addresses Israel as a bride, describing how he found her in her youth and entered into covenant with her:

"And when I passed by you and saw you struggling in your blood, I said to you in your blood, 'Live!' Yes, I said to you in your blood, 'Live!' *I made you thrive like a plant in the field*; and you grew, matured, and became very

---

[105] Sutton, Lecture notes from course on Covenant Theology, Cranmer Theological House, Fall 2012, Weekend One, p. 11

beautiful. *Your breasts were formed, your hair grew;* but you were naked and bare. When I passed by you again and looked upon you, indeed your time was *the time for love,* and *I spread My wing over you* and *covered your nakedness. Yes, I swore an oath to you* and *entered into a covenant with you* and *you became mine,*" says the Lord God.[106]

Then the Bridegroom describes how he anointed and adorned His bride:

"Then I washed you in water; yes, I thoroughly washed off your blood, and I anointed you with oil. I clothed you in embroidered cloth and gave you sandles of badger skin; I clothed you with fine linen and covered you with silk. I adorned you with ornaments put bracelets on your wrists, and a chain on your neck. And I put a jewel in your nose, earrings in your ears, and a beautiful crown on your head. Thus you were adorned with gold and silver, and your clothing *was* of fine linen, silk and embroidered cloth."[107]

He reminds her of how He provided abundantly for her: "You ate pastry of fine flour, honey and oil. You were exceedingly beautiful, and succeeded to royalty. And your fame went out among the nations because of your beauty, for it was perfect through My splendor which I had bestowed on you," says the Lord God."[108]

The entire passage is replete with nuptial terms and speaks of the love of a husband for his bride, of his desire to provide for her and enjoy a beautiful relationship with her.

She did not maintain the exclusive fidelity that He desired, and when we come to Hosea, we find the language of a betrayed husband. Wanting Hosea to provide a picture of what God has suffered in His betrothal to Israel, He tells Hosea: "Go, take yourself a *wife of harlotry* And *children of harlotry,* for the *land commits great harlotry by departing from the LORD.*"[109] This command to marry a woman of ill repute would seem like a very strange edict from God.

---

[106] Ezekial 16:6-8, emphasis mine
[107] Ezekial 16:9-13a
[108] Ezekiel 16:13b-14
[109] Hosea 1:2, emphasis mine

Some commentators have debated whether or not this divinely arranged marriage actually took place or if it is used merely as an allegory to describe God's relationship with Israel. The main issue in Hosea is God's relationship with Israel, not the prophet's relationship with his wife. Jerusalem had become apostate and had violated the covenant with her infidelity, resulting in punishment and separation. She would have to repent and return to her long-suffering husband, who would take her back, forgiving her transgressions and renewing her vows.

> God's reaction to Israel's failure to be faithful is captured in a metaphor, in the dreadful picture of an adulterous relationship and the pain experienced by the betrayed husband.

The story is used to underscore the principles of the covenantal history of God and his people. Hosea's marriage and the names of his children become vehicles for delivering this message. Biblical accounts indicate Hosea was married to Gomer, with whom they had three children. The three children had symbolic names. The first of these was Jezrell, a son whose name was a forewarning of the Lord's vengeance on Jehu's dynasty. A daughter, the second child was name Lo'ruhama, which means "not pitied." The third child, a son, was named "Lo ammi," meaning "not my people." The message from the story was quite clear: Israel was no longer God's people and He was no longer the God of the people of Israel. Despite the fact that the separation was deserved punishment for infidelity, it was not irreversible. The Lord vowed to make available to Israel following her purging and repentance, a "door of hope."[110]

God's reaction to Israel's failure to be faithful is captured in a metaphor, in the dreadful picture of an adulterous relationship and the pain experienced by the betrayed husband (Hosea 2). The Lord tells Hosea to go to his brothers and announce that they are His people and to his sisters that they have received mercy (vs. 1). Then God uses the metaphor, replete with nuptial terms, to describe how Israel has played the harlot and departed from her Husband, the Lord God:

---

[110] Polkinghorn, G. J. "Hosea." *Zondervan Bible Commentary*, ed. F. F. Bruce. Grand Rapids, MI: Zondervan, 1979, p. 873

"Bring charges against your mother, bring charges;
For she is not My wife, nor am I her Husband!
Let her put away her harlotries drom her sight,
And her *adultery* from between her breasts;
Lest I strip her naked . . .
I will not have mercy on her children,
Foor they are *children of harlotry*.
For their mother has played the *harlot*;
She who conceived them *has behaved shamefully*
For she said, '*I will go after my lovers*,
Who give me my bread and my water ....'[111]

The betrayed husband will not tolerate indefinitely this indecency, but will instead intervene and make sure that the adultery does not continue. The metaphor continues with the description of the manner in which he will put a stop to the disgrace:

"Therefore, behold,
I will hedge up your way with thorns . . .
She will *chase her lovers*
But not overtake them,
And she shall seek them;
Yes, she will seek them, but not find them.
Then she shall say,
'I will go and return to my *first husband*,
for it was better for me than now.'
For she did not know
That I [her husband] gave her grain, new wine, and oil . . .
"Therefore I will return and take away
My grain in its time . . . .
Now I will *uncover her lewdness* in the sight of her *lovers*
And no one shall deliver her from my hand. . . . .
And I will destroy her vines and her fig trees,
Of which she has said,
'These are my wages that *my lovers have* given me.' . . .
I will punish her
For the days of the Baals. . . . [112]

[111] Hosea 2:2-5, emphasis mine
[112] Hosea 2:6-13, emphasis mine

And then the faithful Husband, who ever loves and cherishes His bride despite her unfaithfulness, describes how He will restore her and the relationship:

> Therefore, behold, I will allure her,
> Will bring her into the wilderness,
> And speak comfort to her.
> I will give her her vineyards from there
> . . . and a door of hope;
> She shall sing there,
> As in the days of her youth . . ."[113]

The Lord then turns from the metaphor to describe what shall occur in actuality, still using nuptial language:

> "And it shall be in that day," Says the Lord, "That you will call Me *'My Husband,'* and no longer will you call me 'My Master.' . . . . In that day I will make a *covenant* for them . . . I will *betroth* you to Me forever. Yes, I will *betroth* you to Me in righteousness and justice, in lovingkindness and mercy; I will *betroth* you to Me in faithfulness, And you shall know the Lord."[114]

God uses similar nuptial language in Jeremiah to describe the New Covenant:

> "Behold, the days are coming, says the Lord, when I will make a *new covenant* with the house of Israel and with the house of Judah – not according to the *covenant* that I made with their fathers on the day *that* I took them by the hand to lead them out of the land of Egypt, My *covenant* that they broke, though I was a *husband to them,*" says the Lord.[115]

---

[113] Hosea 2:14-15, emphasis mine
[114] Hosea 2:16-20, emphasis mine
[115] Jeremiah 31:31-32, emphasis mine

When we come to the New Testament, again nuptial language is used repeatedly to describe the relationship between the Lord Jesus Christ and His redeemed people: the Church, the Bride of Christ.

Early in the narrative account of Jesus Christ's days on this earth, John the Baptist refers to Him as a bridegroom when explaining the new role that he will take now that the Messiah has become manifest: "He who has the *bride* is the *bridegroom*; but the friend [John the Baptist] of the *bridegroom* [Jesus], who stands and hears him, rejoices greatly because of the bridegroom's voice. Therefore this joy of mine is fulfilled."[116]

Jesus used the image of marriage to describe His own coming again, and the need for his "bride" to be ready, when he told the parable of the ten virgins. The parable is based on the Jewish marriage custom of his day, whereby the bridegroom and his friends left his home and went to the home of the bride, where the marriage would take place. They often went at night, and the bride was expected to be ready to greet her husband. Jesus tells them that the kingdom of heaven will be like

> Jesus used the image of marriage to describe His own coming again, and the need for his "bride" to be ready, when he told the parable of the ten virgins.

> "ten virgins who took their lamps and went out to meet the *bridegroom*. Now five of them were wise, and five *were* foolish. Those who *were* foolish took their lamps and took no oil with them, but the wise took oil in their vessels with their lamps. But while the *bridegroom* was delayed, they all slumbered and slept. And at midnight a cry was *heard*: 'Behold, the *bridegroom* is coming; go out to meet him!' . . . and while they [the ones without oil] went to buy, the *bridegroom* came, and those who were ready went in with him to the *wedding*; and the door was shut."[117]

The parable has numerous applications for being prepared for Christ's coming again; the point for the purposes here is that He used nuptial language to give His warning to be prepared: as God betrothed Himself

---

[116] John 3:29, emphasis mine
[117] Matthew 25:1-10, emphasis mine

to Israel, so we have the picture here of Christ being betrothed to His Bride.

In another instance, when Jesus was questioned why his disciples did not fast, as the Pharisees did, He responded, using nuptial language: "Can the friends of the *bridegroom* fast, as long as the *bridegroom* is with them? But the days will come, when the *bridegroom* shall be taken from them, and then they shall fast."[118]

> We are living in the time between when the Bridegroom has gone to prepare a place for us until when He will return. As surely as He came the first time, He will come again.

Paul frequently refers to Christ as a bridegroom, as, for instance, when he admonishes the church in Corinth with these words: "For I am jealous for you with godly jealousy. For I have *betrothed* you to one *husband* [Christ], that I might present you as a *chaste virgin* to Christ."[119]

Similarly, in writing to the church at Rome, Paul tells them that "Therefore, my brethren, you also have become dead to the law through the body of Christ, that you may be married to another — to Him who was raised from the dead, that we should bear fruit to God."[120]

In his letter to the church in Ephesus, Paul gives instructions to husbands and wives, drawing a parallel between their relationship and the one that Jesus Christ has with His bride, the Church:

> Husbands, love your wives, just as Christ also loved the church and gave Himself for her, that He might sanctify and cleanse her with the washing of water by the word, that He might present her to Himself a glorious church, not having spot or wrinkle or any such thing, but that she should be holy and without blemish.[121]

---

[118] Mark 2:19, emphasis mine
[119] II Corinthians 11:2, emphasis mine
[120] Romans 7:4
[121] Ephesians 5:25-27

**58**

In one of the most beautiful promises Jesus made to His disciples before His departure, He comforted them by telling them that He would come again for them, and in doing so, he used the nuptial language, describing himself as the Bridegroom who would come for His Bride:

> "Let not your heart be troubled; you believe in God, believe also in Me. In My Father's house are many mansions; if *it were* not *so*, I would have told you. I go to prepare a place for you. And if I go and prepare a place for you, I will come again and receive you to Myself; that where I am, *there* you may be also."[122]

We are living in the time between when the Bridegroom has gone to prepare a place for us until when He will return. As surely as He came the first time, He will come again. Those of us who are in liturgical churches proclaim this truth every Sunday in the Eucharist: Christ has died, Christ is risen, Christ *will come* again! (emphasis mine).

In Revelation, we find again the nuptial language to describe what the future holds for Christ's redeemed people, His Bride. John hears the voices of a great multitude rejoicing and saying

> Alleluia! For the Lord God Omnipotent reigns! Let us be glad and rejoice and give Him glory, for the *marriage* of the Lamb has come, and *His wife* is made ready. And to her it was granted to be arrayed in fine linen, clean and bright, for the fine linen is the righteous acts of the saints. Then he said to me, "Write: 'Blessed are those who are called to the *marriage supper* of the Lamb!'" And he said to me, "These are the true sayings of God."[123]

Later John is told to "'Come, I will show you the *bride*, the Lamb's wife' And he carried me away in the Spirit to a great and high mountain, and showed me the great city, the holy Jerusalem, descending out of heaven from God, having the glory of God. Her light was like a most precious stone, like a jasper stone, clear as crystal."[124]

---

[122] John 14:1-3
[123] Revelation 19:6-9, emphasis mine
[124] Revelation 21:9-11, emphasis mine

In the last chapter of Revelation, we see again the "tree of life" (22:2), a reminder of the betrayal in the Garden of Eden, now with everything restored, and the Bridegroom ready for his redeemed Bride. He proclaims, "I am the Alpha and the Omega, *the* Beginning and *the* End, the First and the Last . . . . I, Jesus, have sent My angel to testify to you these things in the churches. I am the Root and the Offspring of David, the Bright and Morning Star."[125] Then we see nuptial language again: "And the Spirit and the bride say, 'Come!' And let him who hears say, 'Come!' And let him who thirsts come. Whoever desires, let him take the water of life freely."[126]

This is

> Liturgical dialogue, a reflection of Eucharistic theology. The Church as bound to God, the bride in union with the Holy Spirit, invites Christ to "Come!" We plead for His return . . . Those who desire God . . . but who are not yet overcoming the world, are in turn invited to come to Christ. [The final words, "Come Lord Jesus"] is a liturgical benediction to the book. The bride, recognizing the voice of her Beloved as He testifies to His Advent, runs out to meet Him . . . and proclaims: Amen . . . come, Lord Jesus! This echoes "Maranatha" (I Cor. 16:22), which was part of the Eucharistic dialogue of the early Church (Didache 10.6).[127]

*The Spirit and the Bride say, 'Come.'*

---

[125] Revelation 22:13-16
[126] Revelation 22:17
[127] *The Orthodox Study Bible*, New Testament and Psalms. Notes on Revelation 22:17-20. Nashville, TN: Thomas Nelson Publishers,1993, 1997, p. 634

# Chapter Four

## GOSPEL OF JESUS CHRIST:
## The Message of the Old Testament

There is little doubt that the early church fathers held that the Old Testament was not contrary to the New Testament, a point articulated firmly by the Articles of Religion adopted in the year of our Lord 1801 by the Protestant Episcopal Church in the United States of America.[128] Redemption and salvation of humanity have been secured and offered by Jesus Christ, our only mediator and advocate with the Father.[129]

Christians believe that there is only one Gospel, for "Nor is there salvation in any other, for there is no other name under heaven given among men by which we must be saved,"[130] and that Gospel appears in the Old Testament as well as in the New Testament. Of this matter, W. O. Carver states that

> without the Old Testament the New Testament could never have been. Given the Old Testament, if its apparent source, significance, and claims were true and genuine, the New Testament had to be. They supplement and explain each other. The Old anticipates the New: The New presupposes and uses the Old. Each part explains and interprets the other.[131]

This position is not without warrant, and the New Testament gives ample evidence that Christ, His apostles, and even His enemies, as well as the Old Testament saints,[132] recognized that the promise of a Redeemer, the Messiah, was contained in the Old Testament.

---

[128] *The Book of Common Prayer*. New York, NY: The Church Hymnal Corporaton, The Church Pension Fund, 1928. Articles of Faith, page 604-611

[129] I Timothy 2:15, I John 2:1

[130] Acts 4:12

[131] Hester, H.I. *The Heart of the New Testament*. Nashville, TN: Broadman Press, 1963, p. 17

[132] Hebrews 11

In preaching the Gospel, Christ and His apostles quoted scripture from the Old Testament as they preached to the masses, and everything they preached came, of necessity, from the Old Testament. One of the most succinct statements in the New Testament concerning this fact is the opening of the letter to the Hebrews

> God, who at various times and in various ways spoke in time past to the fathers by the prophets, has in these last days spoken to us by *His* Son, whom He has appointed heir of all things, through whom also He made the worlds; who being the brightness of *His* glory and the express image of His person, and upholding all things by the word of His power, when He had by Himself[ purged our sins, sat down at the right hand of the Majesty on high ...[133]

The study of the Gospel message as it appears in the Old Testament is extensive, and an exhaustive study of the texts supporting the assertion that the Gospel is contained in the Old Testament is far beyond the scope of this present work.

Instead, I will demonstrate through short passages that Jesus and the evangelists and the writers of the New Testament all testified that God's message of salvation did not begin with the appearing of Jesus Christ on this earth,[134] but rather that it began long before that — began, actually, with the beginning of the history of humanity, in Genesis.

We will then look at two different ways that Christ, or the Messiah, was presented in the Old Testament: through "types" and through direct prophecy.

---

[133] Hebrews 1:1-3

[134] The presentation of Jesus in the proclamation made by John the Baptist shows clearly that the people of his day knew that God had promised a redeemer and that the redeemer would save them from their sins: "Behold the Lamb of God, Who takes away the sin of the world." John 1:36

# The Testimony of Jesus Christ

Jesus Christ accepted the teachings of Jewish scripture, and He and the apostles "considered their work as the completion of God's revelation of Himself to the Jewish people."[135] In fact, Jesus made it clear that He did not come to "destroy the law or the prophets: [but] . . . to fulfill [it]."[136] Christ did not do away with the Old Testament; rather, His life and work were accomplished to explain, clarify, fulfill, and magnify the Old Testament.

On any number of occasions, our Lord Jesus Christ used passages from the Old Testament to substantiate His claims or to proclaim the Kingdom. Christ gave testimony about His purpose on earth, and one example can be seen in a conversation He had with a man named Nicodemus, a Pharisee and ruler of the Jews. After Nicodemus approached Jesus by night and acknowledged that "no one can do these signs that You do unless God is with him," Jesus told Him that no one can see the kingdom of God unless he is born again. To Nicodemus' confused response, "How can a man be born when he is old?" Jesus explained that "That which is born of the flesh is flesh, and that which is born of the Spirit is spirit" and went on to establish His Person and work by using the example of Moses lifting up the serpent in the wilderness, an event that was recorded in Numbers 21. When the people grumbled in the wilderness and spoke against God, He brought fiery serpents that bit them, and many of the people died. After they repented and confessed their sins to Moses, God told Moses to

> "Make a fiery serpent, and set it on a pole: and it shall be that everyone who is bitten, when he looks at it, shall live." So Moses made a bronze serpent, and put it on a pole; and so it was, if a serpent had bitten anyone, when he looked at the bronze serpent, he lived.[137]

---

[135] Hester, p. 17
[136] Matthew 5:17
[137] Numbers 21:8

It was this incident to which Jesus referred when He said to Nicodemus.

> "No one has ascended to heaven but He who came down from heaven, that is, the Son of Man who is in heaven. And as Moses lifted up the serpent in the wilderness, even so must the Son of Man be lifted up, that whoever believes in Him should not perish but have everlasting life." [138]

Jesus obviously was using the Old Testament to make His point and demonstrating thereby that the message of the gospel can be found in the Old Testament.

When asked by the Pharisees about various issues, He would not be tricked by their questions but instead would turn the question back on them by posing such penetrating questions as:

> "Have you not read in the law that on the Sabbath the priests in the temple profane the Sabbath, and are blameless?  Yet I say to you that in this place there is *One* greater than the temple.  But if you had known what *this* means, 'I desire mercy and not sacrifice,' you would not have condemned the guiltless.  For the Son of Man is Lord even of the Sabbath."[139]

In this instance, He quoted from the Old Testament prophet Hosea (6:6), and earlier, He had used the Old Testament account of David and his companions entering the house of God and eating the consecrated bread.[140] The leaders and teachers in Jesus' day believed that they were experiencing a fulfillment of what was foretold in the Old Testament.

When, after His Resurrection He met with the two disciples who were returning from Jerusalem along the Emmaus road and discussing with concern the things which had happened to the one condemned to death and crucified but reported to be alive, Jesus said to them

---

[138] John 3:13-17
[139] Matthew 12:5-8
[140] Matthew 12:3-4; I Samuel 21:6

"O foolish ones, and slow of heart to believe in all that the prophets have spoken! Ought not the Christ to have suffered these things and to enter into His glory?"[141]

Luke goes on to explain that Jesus began at Moses (the Pentateuch, the first five books in our Old Testament) and went through al the prophets, explaining "to them *in all the scriptures* [i.e., Old Testament scriptures] the things concerning himself."[142]

## Testimony of the Evangelists

The Gospels reveal that the evangelists sought to demonstrate that the prophets of the Old Testament times prophesied and promised the coming of the Messiah, the Redeemer of Israel, and that Jesus Christ was the fulfillment of that promise.

Matthew begins his narrative by giving the genealogy of Christ, demonstrating from the very first verse that Jesus is the promised "seed," a matter that will be addressed later. As the "son of David, the son of Abraham,"[143] Jesus is heir to the throne of David and to the promises given to Abraham. Matthew ends the genealogical record by stating "and Jacob begot Joseph the husband of Mary, of whom was born Jesus who is called Christ."[144] From that point, Matthew carefully details the birth, life, death, and resurrection of Christ, repeatedly quoting the Old Testament, showing by proving Jesus was the Messiah that the Gospel was clearly presented in the Old Testament.

Mark begins his Gospel account with the Old Testament prophesy of Malachi, in which he said that one would come and announce the Messiah: "Behold, I send My messenger before Your face, Who will prepare Your way before You: 'The voice of one crying in the wilderness, 'Make ready the way of the Lord, Make His paths straight.'" [145] He is stating that the Gospel he is going to relate, that of Jesus Christ, was already given in the Old Testament. Although he does not quote from the Old Testament as much as Matthew does, he gives several instances

---

[141] Luke 24:25-26
[142] Luke 24:27
[143] Matthew 1:1
[144] Matthew 1:16
[145] Mark 1:2-3; Malachi 3:1

when Jesus quoted from the Old Testament to prove that He was the Messiah and often to rebuke the Jews for not recognizing Him.[146]

Luke writes his Gospel for Theophilus, noting that he is taking care that Theophilus "might know the certainty of those things in which [he had been] instructed."[147] Beginning with the account of John the Baptist's conception, quoting the prophesy from Malachi,[148] Luke then relates the appearance of the angel Gabriel to Mary. In Gabriel's announcement is the reference to the promised "seed": "He will be great, and will be called the Son of the Highest; and the Lord God will give Him the throne of His father David. And He will reign over the house of Jacob forever, and of His kingdom there will be no end."[149] Luke relates Jesus' claim to be the Messiah, noting that the Gospel of salvation was contained in the Old Testament:

> And He was handed the book of the prophet Isaiah. And when He had opened the book, He found the place where it was written:
> "The Spirit of the Lord *is* upon Me,
> Because He has anointed Me
> To preach the gospel to *the* poor;
> He has sent Me to heal the brokenhearted,
> To proclaim liberty to *the* captives
> And recovery of sight to *the* blind,
> *To* set at liberty those who are oppressed;
> To proclaim the acceptable year of the Lord."
> 2Then He closed the book, and gave *it* back to the attendant and sat down. And the eyes of all who were in the synagogue were fixed on Him."[150]

"Today this Scripture has been fulfilled in your hearing."

---

[146] One example was when the Pharisees and the scribes asked Jesus, "'Why do Your disciples not walk according to the tradition of the elders, but eat their bread with impure hands?' And He said to them, 'Rightly did Isaiah prophesy of you hypocrites, as it is written, The people honors Me with their lips, But their heart is far away from Me. But in vain do they worship Me, Teaching as doctrines the precepts of men.'" Mark 7:5-7

[147] Luke 1:3,4

[148] Malachi 4:6

[149] Luke 1:32,33

[150] Isaiah 61:1-2

After Jesus finished reading, He closed the book and said to those who were in the synagogue, "Today this Scripture is fulfilled in your hearing."[151]

In the Gospel of John, we find reference to the preexistence of Christ: "In the beginning was the Word, and the Word was with God, and the Word was God . . . . the Word became flesh and dwelt among us."[152] At the end of the Gospel, after relating many events in the life of Christ, that Word that dwelt among us, John tells that "many other things. . . Jesus did, which if they were written in detail, I suppose that even the world itself would not contain the books which were written."[153] Between those two statements, John gives many examples of how Jesus fulfilled the Old Testament prophesies, and he explains his purpose in providing that explanation:

> And truly Jesus did many other signs in the presence of His disciples, which are not written in this book; but these are written that you may believe that Jesus is the Christ, the Son of God, and that believing you may have life in His name.[154]

## The Testimony of The Apostles

There are many instances of the apostles using the Old Testament to preach the gospel. Perhaps one of the best known ones concerns Philip, when the angel of Lord sent him south "unto the way that goeth down from Jerusalem unto Gaza, which is desert." On his way, he encountered a eunuch from Ethiopia who had great authority in the queen's service and had come to Jerusalem to worship. The eunuch, "a court official of Candace, queen of the Ethiopians, who was in charge of all her treasure," was reading from Isaiah 53. After responding to the Spirit's instruction to "Go near, and join thyself to this chariot," Philip joined the eunuch and heard him reading aloud from the prophet Isaiah,

> "He was led as a sheep to the slaughter;
> And as a lamb before its shearer *is* silent,

---

[151] Luke 4:17-21
[152] John 1:1-14
[153] John 21:25
[154] John 20:30, 31

So He opened not His mouth.
In His humiliation His justice was taken away,
And who will declare His generation?
For His life is taken from the earth."
So the eunuch answered Philip and said, "I ask you, of whom does the prophet say this, of himself or of some other man?" Then Philip opened his mouth and *beginning at this Scripture, preached Jesus to him.*[155]

The eunuch professed his faith in Christ, and Philip baptized him.[156]

> This servant ministry would include not only the Jews but also those from the entire human race.

In another incident recorded in the book of Acts, Stephen made reference to Old Testament prophecy about the coming of the Messiah when he defended himself against the charge of blasphemy. After men from Cilicia and Asia and other parts induced people to accuse Stephen of speaking blasphemous words against Moses and God, the elders, people, and scribes came upon him, seized him, and brought him to the council, where he gave his defense.[157] In that defense, Stephen told his accusers that they resisted the Holy Spirit just as their fathers did, charging them by saying, "Which of the prophets did your fathers not persecute? And they killed those who foretold the coming of the Just One, of whom you now have become betrayers and murders."[158] Stephen, after summarizing the entire history of Israel with regard to the promises given to Abraham, Isaac, Jacob, and David, clearly stated that the prophets foretold the coming of the Messiah and that the One whom they had crucified, Jesus Christ, was that Messiah. He was emphasizing what the Prophet Isaiah had said regarding God's intended plan of salvation for His people: that He would send a servant, the Messiah, to redeem them, "to restore the preserved ones of Israel; I will give you as a light to the Gentiles, that you should be my salvation to the ends of the earth." This servant ministry would include not only the Jews but also those from the entire human race.

---

[155] Acts 8:29-35, emphasis mine
[156] Acts 8:27-38
[157] Acts 6:9-15
[158] Acts 7:52

68

Peter, in his first epistle, makes reference to the prophets, who inquired and serched about the things revealed to them when the Spirit "testified beforehand the sufferings of Christ and the glories that would follow."[159] He also exhorted them to lay aside malice and guile and other faults, explaining that they were living stones, being built up a spiritual house and holy priesthood to offer spiritual sacrifices acceptable to God by Jesus Christ,

> Therefore it is also contained in the Scripture,
> "Behold I lay in Zion
> A chief corner stone, elect, precious,
> And he who believes on Him will by no means be put to shame."[160]

Paul, an apostle called as such by God and an ardent preacher as well as writer, had no access to what we know as the New Testament; in fact, he was responsible for penning fourteen books of it. And in his writing, he repeatedly showed that Jesus was the fulfillment of the Old Testament prophesies concerning the Messiah and the message of redemption.

Paul is known for using the Old Testament in his letters, but perhaps one of the most distinct comments he made regarding the Gospel being found in the Old Testament came when he was giving his defense before King Agrippa. After giving his testimony of his conversion on the road to Damascus,[161] Paul explained that he simply had been following the instructions given to him at that time by the risen Lord Jesus to go to the Gentiles "to open their eyes, *in order* to turn them from darkness to light, and *from* the power of Satan to God, that they may receive forgiveness of sins and an inheritance among those who are sanctified by faith in Me."[162] Then, he declared that, contrary to the charges brought against him, in all his messages, whether in Damascus, Jerusalem, Judea, or elsewhere, he was guilty of

> "saying *no other things than those which the prophets and Moses said would come* — that the Christ would suffer, that

---

[159] I Peter 1:10, 11
[160] I Peter 2:6
[161] Acts 26:12-15
[162] Acts 26:17, 18

He would be the first to rise from the dead, and would proclaim light to the Jewish people and to the Gentiles."[163]

In this statement to King Agrippa, Paul left no question that he considered that the Gospel was presented in the Old Testament and, in fact, that he used only the Old Testament to preach the gospel of salvation.

## Gospel in the Old Testament

Having seen that Jesus Christ, the Evangelists, and the Apostles all testified to the Old Testament presenting the message of the Gospel, let us now look at some examples of that message. We shall look specifically at two literary devices that testify of Jesus Christ and the Gospel. Interwoven throughout the Old Testament, we find both types and prophecies regarding the anointed One, and in those features we also find the Gospel of salvation. The types and prophecies are many, so I will address only a few of the aspects of the Messiah's life, showing the corollary in the New Testament.

### Types of the Messiah

*Passover Lamb*
In the Book of Exodus, God calls from Egypt the person He will use to lead His people, the Israelites, then in bondage in a foreign land, back to the promised land of Canaan. Appearing to Moses, He commanded him to lead his people out of Egypt, through the wilderness, and into Canaan.[164] God sent many plagues to Egypt, but nothing convinced Pharoah to release the Israelites,[165] until the final plague, which caused the death of the first-born child of all those not protected by the divine provision of safety. God told Moses to have the people slay a lamb and take the blood from that lamb and put it over the lintels and the doorposts of their homes. He instructs Moses to warn them that He was going to "pass over" and kill the first-born sons of anyone who was not under the protection of the blood of those lambs. God called this event the "Passover," and He instituted a memorial for the event that is celebrated by the Jews from that time forward.[166] That this event is a type

---

[163] Acts 26:22, 23, emphasis mine
[164] Exodus 3
[165] Exodus 7-10
[166] Exodus 11

of Christ, the Lamb of God, slain for the sins of the world,[167] by whose blood we are saved,[168] is demonstrated in several instances. John the Baptist introduced Jesus as "The Lamb of God Who takes away the sin of the world."[169] He had to be referring to the lambs that were slain as being pictures pointing toward the Lamb.

In our Lord's last Passover meal with His disciples, He took the cup after supper and said to them, "This cup is

> It is important to remember that everyone present was Jewish and that they were commemorating the deliverance God had given their forefathers from their servitude in Egypt.

the new covenant in My blood, which is shed for you."[170] Just before offering the cup, our Lord "took bread and gave thanks, and broke it and gave unto them, saying, "This is my body which is given for you: this do in remembrance of me." He also is referring to His body being given on the cross. It is important to remember that everyone present was Jewish and that they were commemorating the deliverance God had given their forefathers from their servitude in Egypt. Jesus was using that celebration to inaugurate the New Covenant, the shedding of His blood, once for all, for their salvation, or deliverance from the servitude to sin.

*Tabernacle*

While they were in the wilderness, God commanded the Israelites to build a tabernacle where He might dwell among them. The tabernacle also was a type of the Messiah, and that type is fulfilled in the incarnation of Christ. The tabernacle was a tent, as were the dwellings of the Israelites as they wandered through the wilderness, but it was a unique dwelling place of God. It is a picture of Christ, who is fully God and fully man, and dwelt ["tabernacle"] among humanity, as John stated, "And the Word [which "was with God, and . . . was God"] became flesh, and dwelt among us, and we beheld His glory, the glory as of the only begotten from the Father, full of grace and truth."[171] Paul also attested to this fact

---

[167] I John 2:2
[168] I John 1:7
[169] John 1:29
[170] Luke 22:20
[171] John 1:14

when he wrote to the Colossians that "in Him dwells all the fullness of the Godhead bodily."[172]

As the tent itself provided a picture of the Person of Christ dwelling among us, so the furniture in the tabernacle provided many pictures or types of the Person of the Messiah—fulfilled in the Person and work of Christ. First, the *bronze altar*, situated as one entered the tabernacle, is a type of Christ, our substitute and a perfect sacrifice for the sins of humanity. William Brown, in his quintessential study of the tabernacle, quotes from Leviticus to explain that "the altar . . . was to make reconciliation upon, between God and his sinful people."[173] The *laver*, which was used to purify, is a type of Christ as the One who cleanses and brings about regeneration. The altar and the laver can never be separated from one another because without the shedding of blood there can be no cleansing of sin.[174]

The *candlestick* gave light to the tabernacle and was kept burning by pure olive oil. To the believer, Christ provides light and life. He is our source of the true Light, and just as the tabernacle light burned night and day — "perpetually" — in the camp of the Israelites, the light of Christ can never be extinguished. Jesus Himself alluded to this type when He claimed to be "the light of the world" and said that, "He who follows Me shall not walk in darkness, but have the light of life."[175] Another time, He said while healing a man born blind, "While I am in the world, I am the Light of the world."[176] On yet another occasion, Jesus cried out in the synagogue, "I have come as Light into the world, so that everyone who believes in Me will not remain in darkness."[177] One passage is

---

[172] Colossians 2:9
[173] Brown, William. *The Tabernacle: Its Priests and Its Services*. Peabody, Massachusetts: Hendrickson Publishers, 1996, 2002, p. 51
[174] Brown, p. 57
[175] John 8:12
[176] John 9:5
[177] John 12:46

particularly relevant, for it speaks to Jesus' "tabernacling" among them and being the Light to them and also hints at the salvation the Light offers. He said to them,

> "A little while longer the light is with you. Walk while you have the light, lest darkness overtake you; he who walks in the darkness does not know where he is going. While you have the light, believe in the light, that you may become sons of light."[178]

John describes Christ as being life, and says "and the life was the Light men."[179] Later, Peter proclaims Christ's role of calling His people out of darkness into "his marvelous light."[180]

Another piece of furniture in the tabernacle was the *table of shewbread*, and, like the other items, it is a picture of the Messiah fulfilled in Jesus Christ. The Israelites were indebted to God for the gift of bread (the staff of life), and it was their duty to give back a part of what was given to them.[181] The bread on the table was in twelve loaves, representing the twelve tribes; it was to be renewed each Sabbath. Jesus Christ identified salvation and eternal life. He makes specific reference to the bread in the wilderness, the manna that provided sustenance to the Israelites during the journey, when he said

> Your fathers ate the manna in the wilderness, and are dead. This is the bread which comes down from heaven, that one may eat of it and not die. I am the living bread that came down from heaven. If anyone eats of this bread, he will live forever; and the bread that I shall give is My flesh, which I shall give for the life of the world."[182]

His comment was made in response to the grumbling of the Jews because He earlier had said, "I am the bread that came from heaven."[183] In that earlier pronouncement, He had identified Himself in His deity as "the

---

178 John 12:35, 36
179 John 1:4
180 I Peter 2:9
181 Brown, p. 61
182 John 6:48-51
183 John 6:41

true bread," had promised to redeem His people, and had promised to resurrect them:

> "Most assuredly, I say to you, Moses did not give you the bread from heaven, but My Father gives you the true bread from heaven. For the bread of God is He who comes down from heaven and gives life to the world.". . . "I am the bread of life. He who comes to Me shall never hunger, and he who believes in Me shall never thirst. But I said to you that you have seen Me and yet do not believe. All that the Father gives Me will come to Me, and the one who comes to Me I will by no means cast out. For I have come down from heaven, not to do My own will, but the will of Him who sent Me. This is the will of the Father who sent Me, that of all He has given Me I should lose nothing, but should raise it up at the last day. And this is the will of Him who sent Me, that everyone who sees the Son and believes in Him may have everlasting life; and I will raise him up at the last day." [184]

The *golden altar* or altar of incense is yet another type of the Messiah and can be seen with respect to the intercessory role that Christ plays on our behalf. The priests offered prayers and incense at the altar, being a type or picture of our High Priest, who is our only Mediator and Advocate with the Father,[185] who "ever lives to make intercession for us."[186] The writer to the Hebrews explains that these priests, "who offer the gifts according to the law" served as "a copy and shadow of the heavenly things, as Moses was divinely instructed when he was about to make the tabernacle."[187]

Another type of the Messiah we find in the tabernacle is the *mercy seat*, the lid or cover for the ark of the covenant. It represents the forgiveness of our sins, the ultimate propitiation for a fallen humanity. Sacrificial blood was sprinkled on the lid, typifying the shedding of Christ's blood to satisfy the demands of a Holy God and to gain God's forgiveness.[188]

---

[184] John 6:32-40
[185] I John 2:1; I Timothy 2:5
[186] Hebrews 7:25
[187] Hebrews 8:4, 5
[188] Ephesians 1:7

The difference is that He does not, like the priests in the tabernacle, "offer up sacrifices, first for His own sins and then for the sins of the people, for this He did once for all when he offered up Himself."[189] Dwight Pentecost explains this sacrifice was commanded by God so

Another type of the Messiah we find in the tabernacle is the mercy seat, the lid or cover for the ark of the covenant. It represents the forgiveness of our sins, the ultimate propitiation for a fallen humanity.

that the God who must be propitiated could look upon the broken Law contained in the Ark and He could be merciful to men . . . . All this [the sacrifices offered on the mercy seat] anticipated the Lord Jesus Christ, "Whom God hath set forth to be a propitiation through faith in his blood, to declare his righteousness for the remission of sins that are past, through the forbearance of God" (Romans 3:25). What the Apostle is telling us is that when Jesus Christ went to the cross, He gathered together all those notes of indebtedness which the nation Israel had renewed every year on the day of atonement, and he, by the offering up of His blood as that which propitiated a holy God, made a final and complete settlement for all of those notes. As a result there was remission, there was forgiveness of sins that are past. . . . . When we come over to the New Testament we find that the same basic truths which the Old Testament presented in the ritual of the day of atonement are finally and completely fulfilled by the Lord Jesus Christ.[190]

With regard to this sacrifice of "the blood of Christ, who through the eternal Spirit offered Himself without blemish to God,"[191] the writer to the Hebrews also explains that Christ

---

[189] Hebrews 7:27
[190] Pentecost, J. Dwight. *Things Which Become Sound Doctrine*. Grand Rapids, MI: Zondervan Publishing House, 1980, p. 96-97
[191] Hebrews 9:13

came as High Priest of the good things to come, with the greater and more perfect tabernacle, not made with hands, that is, not of this creation. Not with the blood of goats and calves, but through His own blood, He entered the Most Holy Place once for all, having obtained eternal redemption.[192]

## Melchizedek

As our High Priest, Jesus Christ is also likened to Melchizedek, to whom Abraham paid tithes, and is described by the writer to the Hebrews, who explains that "Christ did not glorify Himself so as to become a high priest, but He who said to Him, 'You are My Son, Today I have begotten You'; just as He says also in another passage, 'You are a priest forever according to the order of Melchizedek.'"[193] The writer later explains that

> For this Melchizedek, king of Salem, priest of the Most High God, who met Abraham returning from the slaughter of the kings and blessed him, **2** to whom also Abraham gave a tenth part of all, first being translated "king of righteousness," and then also king of Salem, meaning "king of peace," **3** without father, without mother, without genealogy, having neither beginning of days nor end of life, but made like the Son of God, remains a priest continually.[194]

Of this type, John Walvoord explains that

> Jesus had all the necessary qualities of being a high priest, having been appointed by God himself. . . In his priesthood he fulfilled that which was anticipated in type in Melchizedek, the priest to whom Abraham gave tithes. Like Melchizedek, he had no successors. His ministry and position as High Priest continue forever as indicated in Psalm 110:4.[195]

---

[192] Hebrews 9:11, 12
[193] Hebrews 5:5, 6
[194] Hebrews 7:1
[195] Walvoord, John F. *Major Bible Prophecies*. Grand Rapids, MI: Zondervan Publishing House, 1991, p. 246

In conjunction with this feature, Walvoord also makes the observation that as

> High Priest he offered his own body as a final and complete sacrifice for the sin of the world in contrast to the daily offerings offered under the Mosaic Law . . . In his sacrifice he became our redeemer, our propitiation and our reconciliation.[196]

## Old Testament Prophecies of the Messiah

We also have in the Old Testament the entire story of the Messiah's life, fulfilled by our Lord Jesus Christ. The predictions are found in every book of the Old Testament, and, indeed,

> No other person in history has ever been the subject of the extensive predictions concerning his birth, life, death, and resurrection. Though some passages are devoted to each of these doctrines, the truth concerning Christ's coming is interwoven throughout the Old Testament from Genesis to Malachi. Jesus Christ is the main character of the Old Testament, and understanding this helps one to comprehend the prophecies relating to his death and resurrection.[197]

E. W. Hengstenberg has noted that one can see that the importance of

> the Messianic predictions . . . is manifest from the testimony of Christ and his Apostles. Christ, indeed, declares, that a disposition of mind which qualifies to receive the outward proofs of his divine mission, is indispensable to the knowledge of Himself [John 7:17], and ascribes the unbelief of the Jews to the want of this disposition [John 5:44]. But he also represents the evidence from prophecy as perfectly sufficient in itself; and reproves the Jews because they did not acknowledge it as such [John 5:39-47].[198]

---

[196] Walvoord, p. 246
[197] Walvoord, p. 220
[198] Hengstenberg, E.W. *Christology of the Old Testament and a Commentary on the Messianic Predictions.* Grand Rapids, MI: Kregel Publications, 1970, p. 10

In his monumental work on the *Life and Times of Jesus Christ*, Alfred Edersheim compiled a list of "the passages in the Old Testament applied to the Messiah or to Messianic times in the most ancient Jewish writings. They amount in all to 456, thus distributed: 75 from the Pentateuch, 243 from the Prophets, and 138 from the Hagiographa, and supported by more than 558 separate quotations from Rabbinic writings." He notes that even with considerable care given to this project, "it can scarcely be hoped that the list is quite complete, although, it is hoped, no important passage has been omitted."[199]

What I will provide here is only a brief glimpse at this "story" as told in the Old Testament, but suffice to say that we find that His birth, life, death, resurrection, and ascension all are foretold by the prophets.

### The Seed

In the Book of Genesis, we are told the story of humanity's fall. When Adam and Eve disobeyed God, they lost their spiritual connection. Man became spiritually dead and was separated from God. God promised that just as man had lost that connection, a Man would be born and would reconcile man to God. God began His revelation of the plan of salvation by revealing that the "seed of the woman" would bruise the serpent on the head.[200] This prophesy has been called the "protoevangelium, or the first annunciation of the gospel." Hengstenberg explains that, "As the mission of the Messiah was rendered necessary by the fall, so the first obscure intimation of Him was given immediately after that event."[201]

> God began His revelation of the plan of salvation by revealing that the "seed of the woman" would bruise the serpent on the head.

Stuart Briscoe expands that thought with these words:

> The promised enmity between the seed of the serpent and the seed of the woman not only predicts the promised conflict between Messiah and the demonic forces but also

---

[199] Edersheim, Alfred. *The Life and Times of Jesus the Messiah*. Peabody, Massachusetts: Hendrickson Publishers, 1999, p. 980-981
[200] Genesis 3:15
[201] Hengstenberg, p. 13

gives the earliest hint to the uniqueness of Messiah's birth in the expression "her Seed" when it would be more traditional to talk of the man's seed. The all too common experience of serpents biting men on the heel before being crushed underfoot takes on striking significance when applied to the wounding of Christ through Satan's hostility and the bruising of Satan through Christ's humility.[202]

This first reference to a "seed" was developed later in the Old Testament, beginning when God called Abraham and promised him a son. Paul, writing to the church in Galatia, speaks of the Gospel being preached to Abraham "beforehand." Abraham was a righteous man who trusted in God, and because of his faith and devotion to God, all those of faith would be sons of Abraham. It is through Christ, that the blessings of Abraham come upon the Gentiles: "Now to Abraham and his Seed were the promises made. He does not say, 'And to seeds' as of many, but as of one. 'And to your Seed,' who is Christ."[203] Jesus Christ is the covenant with Abraham fulfilled. He is the ultimate Seed, the spiritual Seed for all Christians. In the book of Revelation, we see God's reclaiming of the kingdom and the redemption of His people and His victory over sin and Satan, fulfilling His covenant with Abraham--the promise of land and a seed.[204]

Genesis reveals more about the Messiah in the reference to the scepter, a symbol of royal authority, not departing from Judah "until Shiloh Comes."[205] Shiloh is an obscure word for one of royal authority, and it can be taken to refer to the Messiah. In Genesis also, the promise is passed on to Abraham's son Isaac and then to Isaac's son Jacob, and later to David.[206] When Matthew wrote his Gospel, he made a point of beginning with Jesus genealogy, showing that Jesus is the "Son of David, the Son of Abraham: Abraham begot Isaac, Isaac begot Jacob."[207]

[202] Briscoe, D. Stuart. *Genesis*. Ogilvie, Lloyd J., ed. *The Communicator's Commentary*. Waco, TX: Word Books, Publisher, 1987, p. 64-65
[203] Galatians 3:16
[204] Genesis 12:1-3
[205] Genesis 49:10
[206] Genesis 12:2,17:19, 21:12, 22:18, 28:14
[207] Matthew 1:1-2

*Birth*

We have already seen that at His birth, Jesus Christ fulfilled the prophecies concerning the "seed" or genealogy of the Messiah. His birthplace was to be in Bethlehem, according to Micah, who said:

> "But you, Bethlehem Ephrathah,
> *Though* you are little among the thousands of Judah,
> *Yet* out of you shall come forth to Me
> The One to be Ruler in Israel,
> Whose goings forth *are* from of old,
> From everlasting." [208]

And, indeed, Jesus Christ was born in Bethlehem.[209]

*Ministry*

Much has been foretold about the life of the Messiah in the Book of Isaiah. The virgin birth was foretold, as was the name He bore, "Immanuel," meaning "God with us."[210] We see another dramatic reference to the Messiah in Isaiah 9, where we are told that "The people who walked in darkness have seen a great light; Those who dwelt in the land of the shadow of death, upon them a light has shined."[211] This is a rather clear statement in support of the Gospel of John, who says of Jesus Christ that "In him was life; and the life was the light of men."[212] The previous verse in Isaiah speaks of the Messiah's ministry being in Galilee among the Gentiles.[213] Matthew demonstrates in several passages (e.g., Matthew 3:13, 4:12) Jesus' relationship to Galilee, and he specifically notes that Jesus is fulfilling Isaiah's prophecy with these words:

> Now when Jesus heard that John had been put in prison,
> He departed to Galilee. And leaving Nazareth, He came
> and dwelt in Capernaum, which is by the sea, in the
> regions of Zebulun and Naphtali, that it might be fulfilled
> which was spoken by Isaiah the prophet, saying:
> "The land of Zebulun and the land of Naphtali,
> By the way of the sea, beyond the Jordan,

---

[208] Micah 5:2
[209] Matthew 2:11
[210] Isaiah 7:14
[211] Isaiah 9:2
[212] John 1:4
[213] Isaiah 9:1

Galilee of the Gentiles:
The people who sat in darkness have seen a great light,
And upon those who sat in the region and shadow of death
Light has dawned."
From that time Jesus began to preach and to say, "Repent, for the kingdom of heaven is at hand."[214]

There are also predictions of a never-ending and greater Kingdom to come, one that traces its line from the House of David: "There shall come forth a rod from the stem of Jesse, and a branch shall grow out of his roots."[215] These are terms (rod and stem) having a Messianic meaning. One of the greatest passages dealing with the future work of the Messiah is addressed in Isaiah where he speaks of the Messiah "swallowing up Death forever" and of the Lord God, Who "will wipe away tears from all faces."[216] In the Book of Revelation, we are told that the tears, which are symbolic of sorrow and pain, will be no more in the presence of God through Christ Jesus, for "God shall wipe away all tears from their eyes; and there shall be no more death, neither sorrow, nor crying, neither shall there be any more pain: for the former things are passed away."[217]

> One of the greatest passages dealing with the future work of the Messiah is addressed in Isaiah where he speaks of the Messiah "swallowing up Death forever" and of the Lord God, Who "will wipe away tears from all faces."

### Trial and Death

Psalm 22 gives a detailed description of our Lord's crucifixion, as does Isaiah 53. For instance, in Psalm 22, we are told that He cried, "My God, My God, why hast thou forsaken me?" These are the very words that Matthew records in his Gospel.[218] In fact, the correspondence between Psalm 22 and Matthew's account of the crucifixion

---

[214] Matthew 4:12-17
[215] Isaiah 11:1
[216] Isaiah 25:8
[217] Revelation 21:4
[218] Matthew 27:46

so literally correspond, that the resemblance cannot possibly be regarded as the result of accident. . . .. It is also manifest that, from among the many words that were uttered, Matthew selected these especially, for the purpose of pointing out the agreement between the prophecy and its fulfillment. Nor is there any doubt that, in bringing forward the remaining circumstances in which this agreement consists, he designed to lead his reader to the conviction, that in the sufferings of Christ, the most remarkable predictions of the Old Testament respecting the Messiah's sufferings, were completely fulfilled.[219]

Isaiah 53 gives a detailed account of the crucifixion, including our Lord's rejection, grief, oppression and affliction, and silence before His accusers, as well as His being an offering for sin. Hengstenberg notes that Jesus Himself attested to this prophecy being about Himself:

The citations of the prophecy in the New Testament serve not only to show, that the Messianic interpretation was the prevailing one in those times . . . but also to furnish us with infallible evidence of its correctness. That the first verse of the fifty-third chapter is cited in the New Testament to explain the unbelief of the greatest part of the people, and with the formula, *'that it might be fulfilled,'* by St. John, would not, it is true, of itself be sufficient for proof. The passage, however, in the thirty-seventh verse of the twenty-second chapter of Luke affords decisive evidence. Christ himself there says, the prophecies relating to Him are *about to have an end*; and that therefore the declaration, *"he was numbered with the transgressors,"* must also be accomplished in Him. –He therefore places the prophecy with those which treat of Himself, and it is certainly so far Messianic as our Lord could know the truth and desire to speak of it.[220]

### Resurrection
Even His resurrection was predicted in the Old Testament, and probably the

---

[219] Hengstenberg, p. 81
[220] Hengstenberg, p. 247-248

most specific prophecy of Christ's resurrection is found in Psalm 16:10: ". . . because you will not abandon me to the grave, nor will you let your Holy One see decay." Though David is speaking here of his own resurrection, the prophecy goes far beyond that of David and refers to Christ.[221]

Knowing that all of these prophecies have been fulfilled, we can say with Job,

> "For I know that my redeemer liveth, and that he shall stand at the latter day upon the earth. And though worms destroy this body, yet in my flesh shall I see God."[222]

## Conclusion

In all these Scriptures, we see that the Old Testament clearly presents the Gospel, both in types and in specific details of the "coming" Messiah. Jesus Christ, as has been declared before, is on every page of the Old Testament.

*We need merely to look, and we will find Him there.*

---

[221] Walvoord, p. 224
[222] Job 19:24, 25

# Chapter Five

# JESUS THE MESSIAH:
## The Priestly Office of Jesus Christ

The Epistle to the Hebrews is recognized as presenting the superiority of Jesus Christ with regard to all that came before Him. Among those aspects is the issue of the great offices held by Christ. The first of these is that of revealer, and another is that of priest. The writer of Hebrews begins by telling us that

> God, who at various times and in various ways spoke in time past to the fathers by the prophets, has in these last days spoken to us by *His* Son, whom He has appointed heir of all things, through whom also He made the worlds; who being the brightness of *His* glory and the express image of His person, and upholding all things by the word of His power, when He had by Himself purged our sins, sat down at the right hand of the Majesty on high, having become so much better than the angels, as He has by inheritance obtained a more excellent name than they.[223]

Later, the writer refers to Christ as an "apostle and high priest of our confession," a twofold ministry.[224]

The Epistle to the Hebrews stands alone in explicitly naming Christ as a priest.[225] In this respect, the writer presents the superiority of Jesus Christ to the entire Aaronic or Levitical priesthood (Leviticus 6:8-8:24) and describes His role as the final High Priest, who offered the perfect sacrifice for all time and has sat down at the right hand of God.[226] It will be the purpose of this chapter to discuss aspects of Jesus' role in this

---

[223] Hebrews 1:1-4
[224] Hebrews 3:1
[225] Vos, Geerhardus. "The Priesthood of Christ in the Epistle to the Hebrews." *Princeton Theological Review*, 5:423-447, 579-604, 1907, p. 604. Available at http://journals.ptsem.edu/id/BR190754/dmd003?page=26
[226] Hebrews 10:12

capacity of High Priest, as presented by Hebrews, drawing on the role described Leviticus.

## Preliminary Matters

Before we approach a discussion of the Lord Jesus Christ as High Priest, a few matters need to be clarified: the background for the priesthood, the assertion that Jesus was a victim, and the contention that Jesus Christ could not have been a high priest.

### Background for the Priesthood

In the early part of Genesis, we learn that Cain and Abel brought sacrifices, perhaps based on the example set by God in the Garden when He shed blood to cover Adam and Eve with skins, following their disobedience.[227] We have no description of an official priesthood that was established during the time of the patriarchs, although Abraham, Isaac, and Jacob offered sacrifices and established sanctuaries in places where significant events in their relationship with God took place. Any mention of priests in the Old Testament usually took place in references to foreign nations.[228]

However, in Genesis 14, a strange occurrence takes place when an individual named Melchizedek[229] appears. The name *Melchizedek* means "king of righteousness." His title as King of Salem [Jerusalem] means "king of peace." Embraced, then, in his name and position or rank are terms associated with Jesus Christ: righteousness and peace. Most interesting is that he is identified as "priest [*kohen*] of God Most High [*El Elyon*]."[230] This is the first mention of a priest in the Bible. We know nothing of his background, but in addition to serving God Most High, he blessed Abram after he rescued his nephew Lot from enemy captivity,

---

[227] Genesis 3:21

[228] Vos, p. 604

[229] In most Masoretic texts, the name is written in two words: *malki zedek*, the former interpreted as meaning "the king" and the latter as meaning "righteous" or "justice." (*Cambridge Bible for Schools and Colleges*, Genesis 14, p. 175, note 18-20). It is thus interpreted in Hebrews 7:2. Philo of Alexandria also referred to Melchizedek as "the one whom God has made as his own priest, a detail which may reflect Ps. 110:4 (*Biblical Figures Outside the Bible*, ed. Michael E. Stone, Theodore A. Bergren;, p. 180. Available at http://books.google.com/books?id=eXM1YwCGipMC&printsec=frontcover#v=onepage&q&f=false)

[230] Genesis 14:18

and he received from Abram one tenth of the plunder of battle, or a tithe.[231] Further, this Melchizedek brought our "bread and wine." for Abram (v. 18), thought by some to be a type of the bread and wine that were on the table of showbread in the Holy place of the Tabernacle/Temple (if the beverage was, indeed, wine) and later that offered by Jesus Christ in the Passover meal that was the precursor to what we celebrate today as the Eucharist.

The short passage is the extent of Melchizedek's appearance in the Old Testament, other than in the Messianic passage of Ps. 110:4. Although the appearance of this priest and king is extremely brief, he plays a significant role in the Scriptures regarding Jesus Christ's position as High Priest. This will become more evident in the discussion on the difference between the Levitical priesthood and Jesus Christ's position as High Priest. An interesting note in all of this is that mono-theism was rare in the ancient world.[232]

> Although the appearance of this priest and king is extremely brief, he plays a significant role in the Scriptures regarding Jesus Christ's position as High Priest.

Much later, after God redeemed His people from bondage in Egypt, He established a priesthood and specific form of worship to be performed by the Levites. The Levites were initially a secular tribe named in Genesis and the tribe from which Moses came. When God called upon Moses to go to Pharoah and release His people, Moses was hesitant to obey the Lord.[233] God then called on his brother Aaron to be Moses' "mouthpiece," and, later, appointed Aaron and his sons to service as priests: "Now take Aaron your brother, and his sons with him, from among the people of Israel, that he may minister to Me as priest, Aaron *and* Aaron's sons, Nadab, Abihu, Eleazar, and Ithamar"[234] It is from this relationship that the Levitical priesthood emerged. It should be noted that not all priests were Levites, though most were.[235]

---

[231] Genesis 14:20
[232] Hawthorne, Gerald F. "Hebrews." *New International Bible Commentary* (ed. F. F. Bruce). Grand Rapids, MI: Zondervan, 1979, p. 1518
[233] Exodus 3:7-4:13
[234] Exodus 28:1
[235] Ross, Allen P. *Holiness to the Lord: A Guide to the Exposition of the Book of Leviticus.* Grand Rapids, MI: Baker Academic, 2002, p. 201

In Leviticus 6:8-7:37 and 8:1-9:24, we have recorded the explicit requirements God set forth for the offerings and the priesthood, which was to be fulfilled by those of the tribe of Levi. We can trace the beginnings of the priesthood in Leviticus chapters 8 through 10. The priestly duties performed by Moses are outlined in the first seven chapters of the book. It says what a priest was to do, and it is from these chapters that Aaron and his son learn to assume their priestly duties.[236] At God's direction, the priestly family was kept separate and distinct from Moses and his descendants, as the priestly office was relegated to Aaron and his sons. In the old order of things, there were different jobs held by distinctively different people. However, in the Epistle to the Hebrews, we see Christ portrayed as shepherd, sacrifice, king, mediator, and apostle.[237]

All of these instructions were given because God intended to set His people apart as Holy. Allen P. Ross says this about the Law:

> The entire law in its final, canonical form is predicated upon the divine plan that the people of Israel were chosen to be a holy nation and a kingdom of priests for God in the world (Exod. 19:5-6). To enable them to fulfill their calling, God gave them this body of regulations and rituals. The regulations guided them into a way of life that put them in sharp contrast with the nations around them, for only when they were set apart from the world would they be useful to God's plan to restore his blessing to the world. And even when they failed to live according to the will of God, they were told that they could avail themselves of the divine provision for full reconciliation in the covenant through the rituals.[238]

With regard to the concept of the priesthood, then, it can be noted that it was not until the Jewish people developed a socio-political structure that

---

[236] Ross, p. 202
[237] Saltau, Henry W. *The Tabernacle and the Priesthood.* GrandRapids, MI: Kregel Publications, 1972, p. 189
[238] Ross, p. 18

a formalized priesthood emerged. The priesthood of the Israelites was more often an office than a vocation.[239]

The most important day of the year was the Day of Atonement[240] (Yon Kippur), when the high priest was to enter the Holy of Holies, and only on that day. The day appointed followed a series of several days, beginning with the first day of the seventh month, when the trumpets were blown to announce the beginning of a new year.[241] The tenth day was the Day of Atonement, and on that day the high priest followed a prescribed ceremony to make an offering for his own sins and then the sins of the people, which involved washings, a ritual with two goats (one slain and its blood carried into the Holy of Holies, and the other led out of the camp and released in the wilderness, never to be seen again, after the high priest placed his hands on it), and changing of his garments (Leviticus 16). The meaning of the two goats is described thus by Warren Wiersbe:

> Remember that the two goats were considered one sin offering (Lev. 16:5). One goat died because there must be blood sacrifice before there can be forgiveness. The other goat lived but was "lost" in the wilderness, having "carried away" the nations sins." He also points out that the "releasing of the goat symbolized the sins of the people being carried away never to be held against them again. 'As far as the east is from the west, so far has He removed our transgressions for us' (Ps. 103:12 NKJV)."[242]

---

[239] Ruscillo, Luiz. *The Priesthood of Christ in the Letter to the Hebrews*. Available at: http://www.faith.org.uk/Publications/Magazines/May09/May09ThePriesthoodOfChristInTheLett erToTheHebrews.html

[240] Wiersbe notes that "the Hebrew word *kapar*, translated "atonement," is used sixteen times in Leviticus 16, and it basically eans 'to ransom, to remove by paying a price." . . . . Atonement means that a price is paid and blood is shed, because life must be given for life (17:11)." He goes on to quote John Stott, who "says it magnificently: 'We strongly reject, therefore, every explanation of the death of Christ which does not have at its center the principle of 'satisfaction thorugh substitution,' indeed divine self-satisfaction through divine self-substitution.'" Wiersbe, Warren W. *The Wiersbe Bible Commentary The Complete Old Testament in One Volume* . Colorado Springs, CO: David C. Cook, 1997, p. 225

[241] Leviticus 23:23-25

[242] Wiersbe, p. 226

**The Assertion that Jesus Christ was a Victim**

Another matter we must consider is the common assertion that Jesus Christ was a victim. Indeed, there are a number of New Testament passages that are seen to highlight Christ's role as victim more than priest,[243] and the concept has been incorporated into today's worship in some Christian traditions. For instance, in the Catholic Prayers, there is the "Litany of Our Lord, Jesus Christ, Priest and Victim," in which Jesus is called upon in these terms: "Jesus, Priest and Victim, Have mercy on us." Among those who describe Christ as both is Fr. Patrick Henry Reardon. He says that

> Whereas in Luke's presentation of Jesus' prayer the Savior appears as the sacrificial victim, in John's presentation he is portrayed, rather, as the sacrificing priest. The relevant text is Jesus' lengthy prayer in John 17. . . . Notwithstanding the subtlety of John's portrayal, Bible-readers have for centuries described the material in John 17 as the "high priestly prayer."[244]

C. H. Spurgeon, too, refers to Jesus Christ as "Priest and Victim," even though he notes the voluntary aspect when he says that

> They dragged the bullocks and they drove the sheep to the altar; they bound the calves with cords, even with cords to the altar's horn; but not so was it with the Christ of God. None did compel him to die; he laid down his life voluntarily, for he had power to lay it down, and to take it

---

[243] Aquinas addresses in Article 2, Objection 1, that "It would seem that Christ Himself was not both priest *and* victim. For it is the duty of the priest to slay the victim. But Christ did not kill Himself. Therefore He was not both priest and victim." Question 22. Aquinas responds that "the slaying of Christ may be considered in reference to the will of the Sufferer, Who freely offered Himself to suffering. In this respect He is a *victim*, and in this He differs from the sacrifices of the Gentiles." http://www.newadvent.org/summa/4022.htm. A better term might be "sacrifice," as victim implies that the one is presented against his/her will, whereas Jesus Christ clearly said, "I lay down my life so that I may take it again. No one takes it from me, but I lay it down of my own accord. I have authority to lay it down and authority to take it up again. This command I received from my Father." (John 10:18, NIV)

[244] Reardon, Fr. Patrick Henry. Christ Jesus – High Priest and Victim. Preachers Institute: World's Premier Online Orthodox Christian Homiletics Resource. http://preachersinstitute.com/2013/02/05/christ-jesus-high-priest-and-victim/

again . . ."For the joy that was set before him, he endured the cross, despising the shame." "He offered up himself."[245]

Despite these arguments, I posit that it is more appropriate to see Jesus Christ as offering Himself as a sacrifice, rather than being a victim. The connotation of victim is that the individual is beset by forces beyond his or her control and forced to do something or to experience something against his or her will. Certainly, neither was the case with Jesus Christ. At any time, Christ Jesus could have been released from the suffering He endured – He was not at the mercy of anyone on earth. Even when Pilate demanded to know why Jesus refused to answer him, saying "Do You not know that I have power to crucify you, and power to release You?" Jesus was under no threat. His response demonstrated that whatever authority and power Pilate might have had, it was no match for Jesus Christ's position: "You could have no power at all against Me unless it had been given you from above."[246] So, we see that the first aspect of the victim, being at the mercy of someone stronger, does not apply to Jesus Christ.

> Despite these arguments, I posit that it is more appropriate to see Jesus Christ as offering Himself as a sacrifice, rather than being a victim.

In the second aspect, being subjected to something against one's will, Jesus submitted His will to the Father's will. This is not to say that He did not struggle, as we see clearly in His anguished prayer in the Garden, "Oh By Father, if it be possible, let this cup pass from Me."[247] But, He always sought to do the Father's will, and so as an act of His own will, He submitted it to the Father's—"nevertheless not as I will, but as You will" — knowing that "for this purpose [He] had come into the world"[248] and that He could trust His heavenly Father, and that beyond the cross was the crown of glory. Jonathan Lunde has this to say

---

[245] Spurgeon, C. H. "Priest and Victim" Sermon #2693. Metropolitan Tabernacle Pulpit, August 28, 1881. Available at http://www.spurgeon.org/sermons/2693.htm (italics added)
[246] John 19:10-11
[247] Matthew 26:39
[248] John 12:27

> By his evocative presentation of his body and blood at the Passover meal, therefore, Jesus is clearly claiming to be the great fulfillment of the gracious sacrifice that led to the exodus and of the redemptive expectations that came later. As such, he is providing in his death the means by which deliverance for the nation will be accomplished again. As Paul declares, "Christ, our Passover lamb, as been sacrificed" (I Cor. 5:7).[249]

Of course, the most important comment is that made by our Lord himself:

> "I lay down my life so that I may take it again. No one takes it from Me, but I lay it down of Myself. I have power to lay it down and I have power to take it again. This command I received from My Father."[250]

Hence, whereas the terms *victim* and *sacrifice* often are used interchangeably, the notion that Jesus did not know what was ahead of Him or that He was a victim of the judicial system or the Jewish religious leaders is simply a misconception at best. As we shall see, as our High Priest, he sacrificed Himself, willingly, "for the joy set before Him."[251]

**Objections to Christ's Priesthood Answered by Aquinas and Apostles**

In his *Summa Theologica,* Thomas Aquinas sets out to answer several questions concerning the validity of the priesthood of Christ, questions that are pertinent to an understanding of Jesus Christ as our High Priest as presented in Hebrews and how that relates to Leviticus.

The first of these questions deals with the issue of whether it is fitting that Christ should be a priest at all.[252] The objection to such is based on a quotation from the Old Testament: "Then he showed me Joshua, the high priest standing before the Angel of the LORD, and Satan standing at his right hand to oppose him."[253] Another objection is that Christ is greater

---

[249] Lunde, Jonathan. *Following Jesus, the Servant King: A Biblical Theology of Covenantal Discipleship*. Grand Rapids, MI: Zondervan, 2010, p. 67

[250] John 10:17, 18

[251] Hebrews 12:2

[252] Aquinas, Thomas. *The Summa Theologica of Saint Thomas Aquinas*. Chicago, IL: Great Books of the Western World (ed., Sullivan, Daniel J.), 1952, Article 1

[253] Zechariah 3:1

than the angels according to Hebrews 1:4, and that it is unfitting that Christ should be a priest because He "was descended from Judah and in connection with that tribe Moses said nothing about priests."[254]

To these objections, Aquinas responds that earlier, in chapter four of Hebrews, there is mentioned Christ's priestly office: "Seeing then that we have a great High Priest who has passed through the heavens, Jesus the Son of God, let us hold fast *our* confession."[255] He also explains that the function of a priest is to be a mediator between God and the people, offering up people's prayers to God and making satisfaction for their sin. He notes that the writer of Hebrews states: "for every high priest taken from among men is appointed for men in things *pertaining* to God, that he may offer both gifts and sacrifices for sins."[256] Such is true of Jesus Christ, who was "appointed by him who said to him, 'You are my Son, today I have begotten you' [and] 'You are a priest forever, according to the order of Melchizedek.'"[257]

In addition to Aquinas' remarks is the explanation that the writer of the epistle makes:

> in the days of His flesh, when He had offered up prayers and supplications, with vehement cries and tears to Him who was able to save Him from death, and was heard because of His godly fear, though He was a Son, *yet* He learned obedience by the things which He suffered. And having been perfected, He became the author of eternal salvation to all who obey Him, called by God as High Priest "according to the order of Melchizedek"[258]

Jesus Christ fulfills the requirements stated above: He offered up prayers and supplications (see John 14 for example), He is a mediator (see also I Timothy 2:5) between God and man, and He became the source of eternal salvation.

---

[254] Hebrews 7:14
[255] Hebrews 4:14
[256] Hebrews 5:1
[257] Hebrews 5:5-6
[258] Hebrews 5:7-10

Peter noted that Christ has bestowed on men all things that are necessary, using as his support these two truths:

> His divine power has given to us all things that *pertain* to life and godliness, through the knowledge of Him who called us by glory and virtue, by which have been given to us exceedingly great and precious promises, that through these you may be partakers of the divine nature, having escaped the corruption *that is* in the world through lust.[259]

Paul, likewise explains that, "in Him all the fullness should dwell, **20** and by Him to reconcile all things to Himself, by Him, whether things on earth or things in heaven, having made peace through the blood of His cross."[260]

Aquinas' remarks are helpful with regard to the priesthood of the old law as a figure of the priesthood of Christ, which was not the same as theirs. He says of Christ's priesthood that

> Christ, as being the Head of all, is the perfection of all graces. Wherefore, as to others, one is a lawgiver, another is a priest, another is a king; but all these concur in Christ, as the fount of all grace. Hence it is written (Isaiah 33:22): "The Lord is our Judge, the Lord is our law-giver, the Lord is our King: He will "come and save us."[261]

Aquinas also addresses the issue of the sacrificial system, stating that man offers sacrifices for three reasons. The first of these is for the remission of sin after having turned from God (Hebrews 5:1). Secondarily, so that man may be preserved in a state of grace. Under the law the sacrifice of these offerings were for the salvation of the offenders as prescribed in the third chapter of Leviticus. And the final reason, so that the spirit of man could be perfectly united to God.[262] The benefits of these offerings are now fully realized to mankind by the humanity of Christ and his perfect offering on our behalf. In Romans 4:24-25, Paul says, "It will be counted

---

[259] II Peter 1:3-4
[260] Colossians 1:19-20
[261] Aquinas, Article 1, Reply to Objection 3, p. 834
[262] Aquinas, Article 2, p. 828

to us who believe in him who raised from the dead Jesus our Lord, who was delivered up for our trespasses raised for our justification."[263]

## Jesus Christ as our High Priest

A key argument in the Epistle to the Hebrews is that Jesus Christ supersedes the Levitical priesthood, even as Melchizedek predated it. In using Melchizedek, that strange character in Genesis, the writer to the Hebrews draws a parallel for the role that Christ plays as our High Priest, saying that He "was designated by God to be high priest in the order of Melchizedek."[264]

The priestly ministry of Jesus Christ is at the heart of the doctrine of salvation. The essence of the Christian faith is found in the twofold aspect of Christ's priesthood, in the incarnation in which he took on our human nature and in the offering of Himself to God the Father on our behalf. As the Son of God, Christ is both fully human and fully divine. In the opening sentence of the Gospel of John, we see echoed the opening phrases of Genesis: "In the beginning was the Word, and the Word was with God, and the Word was God" and then we are told that "the Word became flesh and dwelt among us, and we have seen his glory, glory as of the only son from the Father."[265] The faith of the Church rests on the singular priesthood of Christ, thus presupposing the incarnation and the doctrine of the Trinity. Secondarily, because Jesus is the Son of God, his work of redemption is offered up to God on our behalf as an act of obedience to the Father in the flesh of His own humanity.[266]

> The essence of the Christian faith is found in the twofold aspect of Christ's priesthood, in the incarnation in which he took on our human nature and in the offering of Himself to God the Father on our behalf.

---

[263] *Ibid.*
[264] Hebrews 5:8-10
[265] John 1:1,14
[266] Purves, Andrew. "The Ministry of the Priesthood of Jesus Christ: A Reformed View of the Atonement of Christ." *Theology Matters*, Vol 3, 1997, p. 3. Available at: http://www.theologymatters.com/Julaug97.PDF

## Preparation for the Priesthood

According to Vos, Christ did not officially begin his priestly ministry until he was appointed the "Son of God" and seated at God's right hand. In the "days of his flesh," Christ functioned as an obedient son and, hence, a faithful priest. He argues that Christ's priesthood developed in three distinct stages: the first of these is his incarnation and earthly ministry; the second developed as a result of his crucifixion and resurrection; and the last involves his current reign in heaven and his final glorious return.[267]

A great mystery is the concept that Christ prepared for the priesthood through learning obedience. We are told that during his time on earth, Christ was an obedient son of Israel (Luke 2: 51 – 52; Hebrews 5:8) born under the law (Galatians 4:4). He was the descendant of Abraham and David, both of whom performed priestly duties without a priestly title. He learned the Scriptures (Luke 2:41-52) and dedicated himself to his Father's house. His obedience to his heavenly Father was so great that it consumed him, even as a young lad (Luke 2:49). He was distraught over the abuse of the moneychangers and chased them from the temple (Matthew 21:12-13). Later, after His resurrection, "His disciples remembered that it was written, 'zeal for your house will consume me' " (John 2:17). Emphasizing Christ's divinity, John points out that the Son of God did all he saw the Father doing (John 5: 19-24; 8:38). Jesus' Sonship is a function of his Messianic ministry and, therefore, of His priesthood and Kingship.[268]

Further, being a Son involved learning obedience through what he suffered. The phrase *being a son* can be interpreted in more than one way. It can legitimately be translated, "although he was a son," and some believe it should be "although he was the Son." Their point is that Jesus' unique status as Son of God might have fairly exempted him from suffering and learning obedience. However, even though he had that status, he learned obedience like we do, the point being that a close identification exists between Jesus Christ and those sons and daughters of God who follow in his footsteps. Support for this concept may be found in Hebrews:

---

[267] Vos, p. 579

[268] Hahn, Scott. *Many Are Called: Rediscovering the Glory of the Priesthood.* New York, NY: Doubleday, 2010, p. 278-284

And you have forgotten the exhortation which speaks to you as to sons:

> "My son, do not despise the chastening of the Lord,
> Nor be discouraged when you are rebuked by Him;
> For whom the Lord loves He chastens,
> And scourges every son whom He receives."

If you endure chastening, God deals with you as with sons; for what son is there whom a father does not chasten? But if you are without chastening, of which all have become partakers, then you are illegitimate and not sons. Furthermore, we have had human fathers who corrected *us,* and we paid *them* respect. Shall we not much more readily be in subjection to the Father of spirits and live? For they indeed for a few days chastened *us* as seemed *best* to them, but He for *our* profit, that *we* may be partakers of His holiness. Now no chastening seems to be joyful for the present, but painful; nevertheless, afterward it yields the peaceable fruit of righteousness to those who have been trained by it.[269]

The writer of Hebrews explains that learning obedience through suffering perfected Jesus' earthly ministry. He had become all that a priest could ever be by having learned obedience through suffering and, thus, he was qualified to become the source of eternal salvation for all those who obey him. The application point that the writer is trying to make to his readers is that they should not abandon their faith in Christ because of their suffering. As their great High Priest, Jesus Christ can and does sympathize with them because he, too, has already suffered. With fairness, he could ask them to remain faithful because He had also learned obedience in His sufferings. The constant theme of this letter to the Hebrews is to trust Christ, to obey him, even at the risk of one's life.

The writer further elaborates on the testing of Christ later in the epistle, but here he simply declares that the testing of Jesus was in every respect in the same way that true believers are tested. The word tested could just as well be translated "tempted" in light of the Greek word in the original text. The concept of enticement to sin is part of the meaning. The advantage of the translation "tested" is that it includes both the

---

[269] Hebrews 12:5-11

enticements to sin which do not come from God and the tests that check out our commitment that are permitted and/or actually sent by God.[270]

> Because he experienced the same kind, range, and power of temptations that we experience, he is able to be a sympathetic high priest. Because he did not sin, he is able to be a sympathetic high priest

This should not be understood to mean that Jesus experienced in identical fashion every specific temptation that any of us have experienced. Rather, He experienced the full range of temptation - its full range of power and its full range of areas of life in which temptation occurs. However, there is one important difference between Jesus' temptation and tests, and ours. He experienced those tests and temptations without falling into sin.[271] Because he experienced the same kind, range, and power of temptations that we experience, he is able to be a sympathetic high priest. Because he did not sin, he is able to be a sympathetic high priest.[272]

**Practice of the Priesthood – Meeting the Qualifications**

Before laying out the special qualifications that render Christ a better priest than that provided by Judaism, the author of Hebrews makes some general comments about the qualifications for any high priest (Hebrews 5:1-4). The description is taken from the general expectations of the Old Testament. The author notes that every high priest is human and is appointed by human beings, yet the priest must be called by God. The priest was to represent the people to God and was appointed by people to deal with the things pertaining to God. In this respect, the priest also offered gifts and sacrifices.

Similarly, John Calvin in his commentary on Hebrews describes what he calls four truths about priests from chapter 5. First of all, priests were *taken from among men*. Because of this fact, it was necessary that Christ be

---

[270] Darby, John. *Synopsis of the New Testament*, Hebrews 12. Available on e-sword and at http://www.biblestudytools.com/commentaries/john-darbys-synopsis-of-the-new-testament/hebrews/hebrews-12.html

[271] Hebrews 4:15

[272] *Jamieson, Fausset &, Brown's Commentary on the Whole Bible.* Grand Rapids, MI: Zondervan Publishing House, 1961, p. 1407

a real man. It was the priest who stood in our stead before God. The Son of God has much in common with us and is, thus, fit to reconcile us to God because he walked among us in his humanity. Christ is also a man *for others*. The priesthood was not a private ministry but one that was appointed for the common good of the people. Accordingly, our salvation is connected with and revolves around the priesthood of Christ.

Calvin also notes that we are alienated from God and are in need of a priest who undertakes our cause. That priest is Christ Jesus. In talking about the Levitical priesthood, it is important to note that the priests were to come with *sacrifices to appease God*. A priest without sacrifices is no peacemaker between God and man, for without sacrifice there is no atonement for sin. Christ alone is the only one who can reconcile us to God.

Christ, though free of sin, is a *man who can sympathize*. Everything that applied to the Levitical priesthood did not apply to Christ. Since Christ was free of sin it was unnecessary for Him to offer sacrifice for himself.

Finally, Christ is a "man" by the *call of God*. The lawfulness of any office is dependent on the fitness of the office holder. With regard to priesthood, God makes one fit for that office. Christ and Aaron both have this in common, in that they were called by God. Aaron's priesthood was temporary, whereas Christ's priesthood was perpetual. Christ is therefore a lawful priest appointed by the authority of God.[273]

To look at this matters more explicitly, we will look at the four aspects noted above, comparing how Jesus Christ fulfills and exceeds these qualifications.

---

[273] Calvin, John. *Commentaries on the Epistle of Paul the Apostle to the Hebrews*. (trans., The Rev. John Owen). Grand Rapids, MI: Christian Classics Ethereal Library, Available at http://www.ccel.org/ccel/calvin/calcom44.titlepage.html?highlight=calvin,commentaries,hebrews#highlight, page 96-99 (http://www.ccel.org/ccel/calvin/calcom44.pdf)

## Taken from Among Men and for Men

The Levitical high priest was beset by weakness. He was clothed in or surrounded by weakness. A human priest is also susceptible to sin so that he is obligated to offer sacrifices for himself as well as for his people.[274] Yet, we know that Jesus Christ took on humanity in the incarnation. Of this fact, John speaks eloquently in his Gospel account: "the Word became flesh and dwelt among us." [275] Paul also describes the incarnation in these terms: "who, being in the form of God, did not consider it robbery to be equal with God, 7 but made Himself of no reputation, taking the form of a bondservant, *and* coming in the likeness of men." [276] In writing to Timothy, Paul mentioned His humanity twice: stating that we have one mediator between God and man, he referred to our High Priest as "the man Christ Jesus" and then used the term "manifested in the flesh."[277]

> Yet, in a great mystery, "God made Him who knew no sin to be sin on our behalf that we might become the righteousness of God in Him."

However, as we have already established, using Hebrews 4:15, we know that He was tempted in all ways as we are, yet without sin and that He "committed no sin, nor was any deceit found in His mouth."[278] Yet, in a great mystery, "God made Him who knew no sin to *be* sin for us, that we might become the righteousness of God in Him."[279]

Arthur W. Pink explains the necessity of our Lord's humanity for the redemption of mankind:

> However great the dignity of the substitute, or however deep his voluntary humiliation, atonement for us would not have been possible unless that substitute became actually, as well as legally, one with us. In order to ransom His church, in order to purge our sins, Christ must so unite Himself with His people, that their sins should become His

---

[274] Long, Thomas G. *Hebrews* (Interpretation: A Bible Commentary for Teaching and Preaching). Louisville, KY: John Knox Press, 1997, p. 67

[275] John 1:14

[276] Philippians 2:6-7

[277] I Timothy 1:5, 6

[278] I Peter 2:22

[279] II Corinthians 5:21

sins, and that His sufferings and death should become their sufferings and death. In short, the union between the Son of God and His people, and theirs with Him, must be as real and as intimate as that of Adam and his posterity, who all sinned and died in him. Thus did He, in the fullness of time, assume their flesh and blood, bear their sins in His own body on the tree, so that they, having died to sin, may live unto righteousness, being healed by His stripes.[280]

## Offered Gifts

Specifically, the appointment is to offer gifts and sacrifices for sins. The Greek word for offer literally meant to "bring forward," but it had become a specialized word for the offering of a sacrifice. Given the specific kinds of sacrifices described in Leviticus 1-7, it would be possible to understand gifts as referring to the peace offering and the cereal offerings and sacrifices as referring to the sin and trespass offerings. However, both the context here and the way Jews spoke of the sacrifices in the inter-testament period suggest that the author is simply making a general reference to the offerings that bring atonement.[281]

Martin Luther, in a sermon on Hebrews, addresses the issue of a two-fold priesthood. The former priesthood was of a material nature and dealt with material adornments, tabernacle, sacrifices, and pardons crouched in ritual. The new priesthood was spiritual in nature, with spiritual adornments and a spiritual tabernacle and sacrifices. Of this matter, he says that "Christ, in the exercise of his priestly office, through the sacrifice on the cross, was not adorned in silk and gold and precious stones, but with divine love, wisdom, patients, obedience and all virtues."[282]

The sacrifice offered by Christ was that of His own body and blood, not goats, calves, birds, or bread offered by Aaron and his descendants. Luther points out that even though the body and the blood of Christ were as visible as any other material object, Christ's sacrifice was more spiritual than material: "Christ offered himself in the heart before God." Furthermore he states that this true sacrifice was perceptible to no mortal

---

[280] Pink, Arthur W. *An Exposition of Hebrews.* Grand Rapids, MI: Baker Book House, 1953, p. 147

[281] Long, p. 67

[282] Luther, Martin. "Christ Our Great High Priest." *The Sermons of Martin Luther*, Vol. VII, p. 163. Available at: http://www.sacred-texts.com/chr/luther/highpre.htmp

and that his body and blood became a spiritual sacrifice. Likewise, when Christians offer up their own bodies as in Romans 12:1, it is a spiritual sacrifice that St. Paul refers to it as "reasonable service."[283]

Luther also points out that Christ was offered on a cross and, therefore, not in a temple. It was an offering before the eyes of God, and the altar in a "spiritual sense" was the cross. The effects of the Old Covenant's sacrificial system were ineffectual to say the least. The absolution received by sinners rendered no one inwardly holy or just before God. It is through the priesthood of Christ that true spiritual remission, sanctification and absolution takes place. The writer to the Hebrews says that

> But Christ came *as* High Priest of the good things to come,[a] with the greater and more perfect tabernacle not made with hands, that is, not of this creation. Not with the blood of goats and calves, but with His own blood He entered the Most Holy Place once for all, having obtained eternal redemption.[284]

> As a result of Christ's coming to the cross on our behalf, we are owners of the blessings wrought by him, both spiritual and eternal.

As a result of Christ's coming to the cross on our behalf, we are owners of the blessings wrought by him, both spiritual and eternal. Luther concludes his sermon by making note of the fact that in Leviticus 16, the high priest must once a year entered into the holy place with the blood of rams and other offering, and with these make formal reconciliation on behalf of the people. Christ, the true high Priest, made for us a once true and holy sacrifice on our behalf for the remission of sins. Under the old economy of the Jewish sacrificial system, those offerings had to be repeated every year. Under the old dispensation, the transgressions of man remained, but through Christ, our "only mediator and advocate", our sins are washed away through his blood.[285]

We see that Christ, in performing his priestly duties, offered up his death as an unblemished sacrifice to God; and in doing so becomes a priest

---

[283] Luther, p. 164
[284] Hebrews 9:11, 12
[285] Luther, p. 167

suspended between heaven and earth. Because Christ is active in this act, it is clear that he is functioning as a priest not merely as a sacrifice. His death by crucifixion fulfills the role of "priest" and "sacrifice". Christ is a man metaphysically speaking and is metaphorically a lamb.[286]

In the Gospel of John, we read these words from Jesus Christ:

> "I am the good shepherd. The good shepherd gives His life for the sheep. But a hireling, *he who is* not the shepherd, one who does not own the sheep, sees the wolf coming and leaves the sheep and flees; and the wolf catches the sheep and scatters them. The hireling flees because he is a hireling and does not care about the sheep. I am the good shepherd; and I know My *sheep,* and am known by My own. As the Father knows Me, even so I know the Father; and I lay down My life for the sheep."[287]

Later in that chapter, Christ expands his mission to include ministry to the Gentiles by saying "And other sheep I have which are not of this fold; them also I must bring, and they will hear My voice; and there will be one flock *and* one shepherd."[288]

> The high priest also had to be able to deal gently with the ignorant and the erring ones.

### Had Sympathy for the People

The high priest also had to be able to deal gently with the ignorant and the erring ones. It was important that the high priest not only carry out the performance of the rituals with precision and dignity; he was to have the inward sympathy and discernment to know how to deal with each individual according to that person's needs. The term to "deal gently" with someone means to restrain, control, and change one's own feelings. It speaks of tolerance and an understanding of the range and reality of real human problems but is not indulgent of that which offends God. A priest who was repulsed by rather typical human failings would not be able to help the person because of his own disgust for them. [289]

---

286 Purvis, p. 1
287 John 10:11-15, emphasis mine
288 John 10:16
289 *Ibid.*

The ability to deal sympathetically and yet in a redemptive manner is directed toward those who are ignorant, as well as those who sin. This way of describing those needing the help of the priest appears to arise from Leviticus 4:1-5 and 6:24-30. Also, we find these words in Numbers 15:27-31, where the Law is restated: "If one person sins unintentionally, he shall offer a female goat a year old for a sin offering. And the priest shall make atonement before the LORD for the person who makes a mistake, when he sins unintentionally, to make atonement for him, and he shall be forgiven." An important distinction is made between those who sin unwittingly - by error and/or ignorance - and those who sin "with a high hand" - arrogantly and presumptuously acting against God.[290, 291]

Not only did Christ demonstrate the high priestly quality of humility, but He also demonstrated sympathy, as verse 7 states. He offered prayer and supplications with loud cries and tears. The mention of prayer and supplications implies a closer relationship with God than that characterized by "gifts and sacrifices." The sympathy that Hebrews 5:3 had described is reflected in loud cries and tears. The author's main point is to show the ability of Jesus to sympathize with us:

> "For we do not have a High Priest who cannot sympathize with our weaknesses, but was in all *points* tempted as *we are, yet* without sin. Let us therefore come boldly to the throne of grace, that we may obtain mercy and find grace to help in time of need."[292]

### Called by God
That intensity of identification with a sinful people means that no priest presumes to take this honor of his own accord. Though the appointment to the priesthood is by human beings according to verse 1, the call or summons to the priestly role is from God. No one in his or her right mind seeks the privilege of building bridges from humankind to God. To represent the people of God is by all rights a stretch. To represent God to the people is a task too great to seek. One must be called by God.[293]

---

[290] Keil C.F. "The Pentateuch." *Keil & Delitzsch Commentary on the Old Testament*. Vol 1. Peabody, MA: Hendrickson Publishers, Inc., p. 721
[291] Constable, p. 21, 76
[292] Hebrews 4:15, 16
[293] Long, p. 69

> Just as every high priest humbly did not seek the office, so Christ humbly did not glorify himself in becoming our High Priest but was appointed.

Just as every high priest humbly did not seek the office, so Christ humbly did not glorify himself in becoming our High Priest but was appointed. The concept of glory is mentioned several times in Hebrews. For instance, the writer quotes the Old Testament in establishing "you made him for a little while lower than the angels; You have crowned him with glory and honor, And set him over the works of Your hands. You have put all things in subjection under his feet." [294] Later, the author states that Jesus was "worthy of more glory than Moses."[295] The author then quotes Psalm 2:7, "You are my Son, today I have begotten you."

Constable notes that no further argument was thought necessary since the author had already quoted this verse in Hebrews 1:5.[296]  However, we might add that, with regard to being called of God, we know from John 3:16 that the Father sent the Son into the world, that Jesus did that which he saw the Father doing (John 5:19), and that He did not speak of His own accord but of what the Father commanded (John 12:49).

### Perfection of the Priesthood – After the Order of Melchizedek

Christ becomes the fulfillment of that which Aaron had foreshadowed as the high priest of his people. In the Hebrews 5:11 Christ is declared as a high priest after the order of Melchizedek, which preceded the Law and had nothing to do with the Levitical priesthood.

The next two chapters of Hebrews concern themselves with showing how Christ is a superior priest when compared to the Jewish priesthood. The author points out that Melchizedek was greater in his person than Aaron, and that this superiority was apparent in comparison to the entire Levitical stock.[297] Jesus did not emerge from the tribe of Levi but from the

---

[294] Hebrews 2:7-8a
[295] Hebrews 3:3
[296] Constable, Thomas I. *Notes on Leviticus*. (2013 Edition) p. 47. Available at
   http://soniclight.com/constable/notes/pdf/leviticus.pdf
[297] Pink, p. 380

Royal tribe of Judah. The priesthood of Jesus Christ parallels that of Melchizedek in that he was both King and Priest.[298]

Jesus Christ is compared to Melchizedek in the seventh chapter of Hebrews in these words:

> Therefore, if perfection were through the Levitical priesthood (for under it the people received the law), what further need *was there* that another priest should rise according to the order of Melchizedek, and not be called according to the order of Aaron? For the priesthood being changed, of necessity there is also a change of the law. For He of whom these things are spoken belongs to another tribe, from which no man has officiated at the altar. For *it is* evident that our Lord arose from Judah, of which tribe Moses spoke nothing concerning priesthood.[299]

The Jewish people believed the Law to be the final word of God. There was also an assumption that the Aaronic priesthood was superior to that of Melchizedek's and was thought to be God's way of replacing all previous priesthoods. The author of Hebrews points out that the priesthood of Melchizedek was spoken of in Psalm 110, long after the giving of the Law. Therefore, the priesthood of Aaron was incapable of accomplishing its intended purpose. [300]

## The Superiority of Our High Priest

Christ's superior priesthood is illustrated by his cleansing of the temple, in his upholding of the law, by His teaching, His offering himself up as a sacrifice, and His mediation of the new covenant. Christ in his person and work, and His identification as the Son of Man is a far better Priest then the Israelite priesthood that is found in the Old Testament and in the Gospels.

---

[298] Morris, Leon. *Expositor's Bible Commentary*, Vol. 12. Grand Rapids, MI: Zondervan, 1981, p. 66

[299] Hebrews 7:11-14

[300] Pink, p. 381

The priests in Jesus' day continually defiled the temple with their impure your hearts. Jesus cleansed the temple and rebuked them for their self-righteousness, saying

> "Do you not yet understand that whatever enters the mouth goes into the stomach and is eliminated? But those things which proceed out of the mouth come from the heart, and they defile a man."[301]

The Levitical priesthood attempted to bring about man's acceptability before God, but as the author of Hebrews states, it was incapable of doing so. In looking at the connection between the priesthood and the Law, a change in one, means a change in the other.[302] The priesthood of Melchizedek, therefore, differed fundamentally from that of the Aaronic priesthood. Likewise, the priesthood of Christ is both different and better. The Law was the basis for the Aaronic priesthood, and when the Law gave way, its priesthood lost the basis for its existence. One of the reasons for the change in the Law is the fact that Jesus did not belong to a tribe recognized as having a priestly role. No one of the tribe of Judah had ever attended to the altar. Moses had nothing to say about priests, and no one imagined the priesthood from any tribe other than the Levites. Likewise there was no reason for introducing a newer and better priesthood if the old one met all of the requirements established by God.[303]

In addressing the issue of perfection, Arthur W. Pink states that perfection simply means bringing a person or thing to completeness for that which it was ultimately created. With regard to Christian doctrine, perfection refers to producing a right relationship between God and man. Since perfection could not be produced by the Levitical priesthood, it stands to reason that a priesthood that brings about such a result must be superior. [304]    According to Hughes, Christ's superior and eternal

---

[301] Matthew 15:17, 18
[302] Morris, p. 67
[303] Morris, p. 67
[304] Pink, chapter 32

priesthood after the order of Melchizedek, was affirmed in Psalm 110:4 and quoted in Hebrews 7:20-23, and established by an oath. He explains that

> For those who formally became priests were made such without an oath, but this one was made a priest with an oath by the one who said to him: "the Lord has sworn and will not change his mind, you were a priest forever." This makes Jesus the guarantor of a better covenant. The former priests were many in number, because they were prevented by their mortality from continuing in their office, but Christ holds his priesthood permanently, because he continues forever. Consequently, he is able to save to the uttermost those who draw near to God through him, since he always lives to make intercession for them.[305]

**Likewise, Christ is the sole mediator between God and man.**

Christ, therefore, becomes the guarantor of a newer and better covenant. Christ makes constant intercession for us in heaven. And, according to Hughes, is always "infallible in its effectiveness." Likewise, Christ is the sole mediator between God and man. Under the old system sacrifices were offered repeatedly. The sacrifice made by Christ was offered but once, never to be repeated, unlike the old external and superficial sacrifices made by the Levitical priesthood on a regular basis.[306]

## Christ's Prevailing Priesthood

Is the work of Christ finished? The study of salvation, or soteriology, can be viewed as an accomplished and completed work in a historical context but also seen as ongoing because of the benefits that are always being bestowed on individuals throughout time. There is no doubt that when Christ cried out on the cross that "it is finished" (John 19:30) that it was in reference to his completed work on the cross.

---

[305] Hughes, Phillip Edgcombe. *Commentary on the Epistle to the Hebrews*. Grand Rapids, MI: Wm. B. Erdmons Publishing Company, 1977, p. 234
[306] Hughes, p. 354

The work of Christ as our High Priest, who offered Himself as the eternal sacrifice for our sins, was pleasing to the Father, who

> has highly exalted Him and given Him the name which is above every name, that at the name of Jesus every knee should bow, of those in heaven, and of those on earth, and of those under the earth, and *that* every tongue should confess that Jesus Christ *is* Lord, to the glory of God the Father."[307]

The encouragement we experience because of Christ's High Priesthood is outlined in the chapter four of Hebrews. The author begins this section by stating that we have a great high priest who has passed through the heavens. What is meant by the phrase that Jesus Christ has passed through the heavens is not clear. Some people take it to mean that Jesus Christ has passed on into the heavenly rest that was discussed in the earlier verses of chapter 4. It is also possible to see the phrase as a reference to the Incarnation. Jesus has passed through the heavens as he made his journey to earth to live and die among us. The first meaning may be most likely in the total context of Hebrews. It is consistent with the idea of Jesus has passed through the heavens to the throne of God. We will eventually follow him on that journey. Having arrived in heaven, He is now at the right hand of God interceding for his people (Hebrews 4:14-16).

> The role of Jesus now in heaven interceding for and inviting the readers of Hebrews to follow makes it imperative that they remain true to Christ.

Because Jesus is both interceding for us and inviting us to follow in his footsteps the author can make this exhortation, "let us hold fast the confession." The exact content of the confession is not stated, but it must refer to the affirmation of the basic elements of the Christian faith. The role of Jesus now in heaven interceding for and inviting the readers of Hebrews to follow makes it imperative that they remain true to Christ. The writer looks at the work of our high priest who is at the throne of God and is there on behalf of the faithful interceding for them. The

---

[307] Philippians 2:9-11

message is clear: that turning back from trust in Christ makes no sense at all for the author of Hebrews.[308]

The writer turns in verse 15 from a positive affirmation to a negation. We do not have a high priest who is unable to sympathize with our weaknesses. Positively stated, we do have a sympathetic high priest in Christ. The word sympathize comes directly from a Greek word with roots meaning "to feel with." Christ is able to feel with us in our feelings of weakness, fear, anxiety, insecurity, and being torn between choices that are complicated and difficult. He feels with us and for us in those circumstances because he has been tested in every way like we have been.[309]

The author concludes that we should draw near to the throne of grace with confidence and boldness to receive mercy in time of need (Hebrews 4:16). We will not find rejection and mocking. We will find mercy and timely help. Because Jesus has experienced all the pain and divergent pulls of life, he is both qualified and eager to give us help at the right time and in the right way.[310]

I am reminded of the lyrics of a song by Philip B. Bliss[311] that sums up the work of our Great High Priest:

> "Man of Sorrows!" what a name
> For the Son of God, who came
> Ruined sinners to reclaim.
> Hallelujah! What a Savior!
>
> Bearing shame and scoffing rude,
> In my place condemned He stood;
> Sealed my pardon with His blood.
> Hallelujah! What a Savior!
>
> Guilty, vile, and helpless we;
> Spotless Lamb of God was He;

---

[308] JFB, p. 1407
[309] Ibid.
[310] Barnes, Albert. *Notes on the New Testament* (ed., Frew, Robert). Grand Rapids, MI: Baker Books, 1884-85, 2001, p. 107
[311] Can be heard here: http://www.youtube.com/watch?v=bsYaVG2cgak

"Full atonement!" can it be?
Hallelujah! What a Savior!

Lifted up was He to die;
"It is finished!" was His cry;
Now in Heav'n exalted high.
Hallelujah! What a Savior!

When He comes, our glorious King,
All His ransomed home to bring,
Then anew His song we'll sing:

*Hallelujah! What a Savior!*

## Chapter Six

# CHRISTIAN SPIRITUALITY
## A Comparison of Different Traditions

The term "Spirituality" is tossed about today, as it was in the past, in different quarters with a wide variety of meanings. How one defines it is seen in the different approaches to spirituality, which see it in various terms ranging from ethics and morality to theological reflection to communication with spirits, as well as in terms of prayer, meditation and other spiritual practices, including for some healing and psychological growth. In an attempt to clarify the meaning of the term, Crumley et al. look at the etymology of the word, noting that the Hebrew *ruah*, Greek *pneuma*, Latin *spiritus*, and Sanskrit *prajna* all mean both "breath" and "spirit." In this sense, spirituality

> is the wellspring of our sense of meaning and of our will to live, the source of our deepest desires, values and dreams. . . . not a thing apart from our daily lives, but rather the fundamental energy source that fuels all our emotions, relationships, work, and everything else we consider meaningful. Contrary to popular belief, spirituality is not something special or extraordinary. It is instead absolutely ordinary and completely natural.[312]

William Wolf, in *Anglican Spirituality*, says that "the word suffers from indeterminancy at its edges, but it is used to describe practice that makes religion come to life." According to Wolf, spirituality is nothing more nor less than "piety" or "devotion" that directs one's life, one's entire existence, into prayer, worship, and discipline. Hence, our spirituality involves *how we live in the Spirit*, giving form and texture to our Christian life.[313]

---

[312] Crumley, Carole, Bill Dietrich, Ann Kline, and Gerald May. Contemplative Spirituality. Shalem Organization. Available at
http://www.shalem.org/resources/publication/articles/contemplativespirituality.html
[313] Wolf, William. "Introduction." *Anglican Spirituality*. Wilton, CN: Morehouse-Barlow Co., Inc., 1982, p. iv

If we were to contrast spirituality to theology, we could say that theology deals with what we believe and how we believe it, whereas spirituality involves our practice and action. When we speak of spirituality, we must look at how one opens oneself to the power of the Holy Spirit.

*. . . our spirituality involves how we live in the Spirit, giving form and texture to our Christian life.*

Hence, spirituality is interpreted and defined differently according to the type of church to which one belongs. Guthrie suggests three basic types of churches. The first is the *confessional church,* one in which its members make a confession of faith (common faith). The second is the *experiential church,* which holds that one becomes part of the Church by a conversion process, having been saved by an acknowledgement of Christ Jesus as personal Lord; within this category, many people undergo a similar religious experience. The third type is the *pragmatic church,* one in which its members are engaged in common liturgical and sacramental practices. Member of this third type of church undergo baptism, participate in the Eucharist, and observe religious practices or ordinances. In this last group of churches, members may have had different religious experiences or none at all and may or may not hold to the same doctrinal positions.[314] This chapter examines forms of spirituality as they are defined and practiced by the Lutheran, Methodist, Pentecostal, and Reformed churches, as well as the "contemplative" approach, ending with a discussion on particular aspects of Anglican spirituality.

## Lutheran View of Spirituality.

One approach to Lutheran spirituality is presented by Gerhard O. Forde, who places great emphasis on theological aspects. According to this approach, a primary consideration for Lutherans is the doctrine of sanctification, which is described as the "art of getting used to justification, a work of the Holy Spirit."[315] Sanctification in this sense is seen as separate from justification by virtue that God is doing His part

---

[314] Guthrie, Harvey H. "Anglican Spirituality: An Ethos and Some Issues" in Wolf, William J. (ed), *Anglican Spirituality.* Wilton, CN: Morehouse-Barlow Co., Inc., 1982, p. 3

[315] Forde, Gerhard O. "The Lutheran View" in Alexander, Donald L. (ed). *Christian Spirituality: Five Views of Sanctification.* Downer's Grove, IL: InterVarsity Press, 1988, p. 14

and we are doing our part. Justification is by faith, but it requires that we think in terms of the death of the old self and the resurrection of the new self. [316]   Hence, our sanctification cannot be separated from our justification, and, indeed, one who is not being sanctified is not, or has not been, justified.[317]

This position is based on the words of St. Paul in his letter to the church in Corinth: "To the church of God which is at Corinth, to those who are sanctified in Christ Jesus, called to be saints, with all who in every place call on the name of Jesus Christ our Lord, both theirs and ours" (I Corinthians 1:2).   In this passage, St. Paul states that those called to be saints are sanctified in Christ Jesus.  Similarly, one is saved "through the sanctifying work of the Spirit" (II Thessalonians 2:13),[318] based on the fact that, according to the letter to the Hebrews, we are "sanctified through the offering or body of Jesus Christ once and for all."[319]

> Justification is by faith, but it requires that we think in terms of the death of the old self and the resurrection of the new self.

For Forde, this emphasis on justification is expressed especially in the Lutheran concept of spirituality, which is seen through the lens of the saving work of Christ Jesus…leading to justification by faith alone, whereby one becomes justified through the work of Christ. "Because" of Jesus' death and resurrection, we "therefore have been saved." "Because" Jesus has borne the sin of the world, we "therefore" have forgiveness of our sins.[320]

In this particular Lutheran view of spirituality, Christians begin a new life by being baptized into Jesus, thus baptized into his death.  According to Romans 6:1-11, because of Christ's death, we can count ourselves dead to sin but also alive to God; we no longer are slaves to sin because of our new birth into Christ Jesus.  We become new beings, the old self has died, and the new self is the recipient of "unconditional justification," and the

---

[316] Ibid., p. 15
[317] Ibid., p. 16
[318] Ibid., p. 17
[319] Ibid., p. 17
[320] Ibid., p. 18-19

"grace itself slays the old self and destroys the body of sin, so as to fashion a new one"[321]

Spirituality, then, is part of our sanctification, "a matter of being grasped by the unconditional grace of God and having to live in that light."[322] Justification is by faith alone and is part of the unconditional promise that brings us to sanctification; the key term is *unconditional* in that it "grants everything all at once to the faith that it creates."[323] Forde points out that Luther says we are "simultaneously just and a sinner" because of the grace of God.

In this particular Lutheran view of spirituality, Christians begin a new life by being baptized into Jesus, thus baptized into his death.

The first step toward sanctification in this position is to realize that we are sanctified. He asks, "How do we stand outside of this state? The first possibility is that we have not responded properly; the second is that God has chosen not to give us His divine grace. Hence, Christians live in a state in which sin and righteousness exist side by side.[324] Because our righteousness cannot be gained through the Law and there is nothing that we can do to secure it by our own works, the first step towards sanctification comes from putting it back into God's hands. Forde further notes Luther's view that progress in the area of sanctification is the work of grace because we are justified by grace alone.[325]

The second part of this equation, according to Forde, is that we are not moving toward some goal but that it moves toward us. This is a restatement of the idea that we are powerless to act on our own in securing our sanctification. We do not grow in grace by our efforts. The progress we make as Christians depends on our ability to lose sight of our self and submit to the saving grace of God. He goes on to state that the Lutheran view tells us that one is likely to engage in truly good works as a result of fruits of one's sanctification. These works would be actions or deeds that the individual would most likely not remember. Another of

---

[321] Ibid., p. 21
[322] Ibid., p. 22
[323] Ibid., p. 23
[324] Ibid., p. 25
[325] Ibid., p. 26

these acts would be "taking care" of "our neighbor and God's creation." In "taking care," one would engage in such activities not as a means of securing sanctification but because one already is sanctified. In another area, vocation, Christians would tend to carry out the tasks and vocations of daily life for the greater honor and glory of God. Truthfulness and lucidity are the ways in which Lutherans should address the progress or lack thereof in everyday Christian life, causing one to realize that our salvation is by the grace of God alone.[326]

Another aspect of Lutheran spirituality, perhaps the "getting used to justification," is offered by Andrew F. Weisner, college pastor of Lenoir-Rhyne College in Hickory, North Carolina. He states that "there is a specific Lutheran spirituality. It is not uniquely Lutheran, because Christians of other traditions practice styles of spirituality similar to it. But there is a 'Lutheran form,' which is readily accessible to any seeker."

For Weisner, the "building blocks," or "rather, the very foundation, for this Lutheran form of spirituality are found in the *Lutheran Book of Worship* (1978) and the Augsburg Fortress supplementary worship resource." Using the words from the final verse of Martin Luther's hymn, *A Might Fortress is Our God*, Weisner points out that the "weapons of the Spirit" are the preaching of the Word of God, baptism, confession and forgiveness, the holy Eucharist, daily prayer, and the singing of psalms and hymns and spiritual songs."

He supports this position by reiterating that these actions are "foundations for a 'Lutheran spirituality'" and notes that in the most basic, well-known document of Lutheranism, the Small *Catechism*, Luther exhorts and intends that "the faithful observe all of these activities (with the exception of singing; Luther does not mention 'singing' . . . [but] obviously considered singing to be valuable, since he composed so many hymns, liturgical and otherwise, for people's use." He concludes his remarks, which follow a detailed explanation of how the college provides opportunities to fulfill the "building blocks" he has enumerated, by stating that "Young people are looking for some thing, or Someone, to whom they can commit—or even, abandon—themselves. Talk of spirituality and efforts toward spiritual formation at our Lutheran

---

[326] Ibid.

colleges should tell them about, show them, and sacramentally, incarnationally, give them Jesus." [327]

## Methodist View of Spirituality

The Methodist view of spirituality emerges from eighteenth century England and the church's founder, John Wesley. It incorporates much of what we will see in Anglican spirituality, a result no doubt of Wesley having been an Anglican priest. Wesley believed that spirituality should include "the means of grace" or "works piety." The means of grace included a prayer life that involved daily private devotions (morning and evening prayer). In one's prayer life should be included a way of expressing love and gratitude to God. It should also include regrets for our failure to love and serve others. Wesley encouraged followers to tell God about their thoughts and feelings, as well as make requests to God, intercessory prayers, and listen to God for guidance and correction. In addition to daily prayer, Wesley also encouraged daily reading of the Scriptures, which was to be done seriously, systematically, and carefully with prayer.

> Early Methodist practices included frequent worship and sharing in the Lord's Supper as often as possible as a means of union with Christ and fellow Christians.

Early Methodist practices included frequent worship and sharing in the Lord's Supper as often as possible as a means of union with Christ and fellow Christians. Fasting also was encouraged at least once a week, during Wesley's time. In reference to the Bible, Wesley, like Anglicans, believed that it should be interpreted through experience, tradition, and reason.[328]

An important element in Wesleyan spirituality is the process of "becoming." For the Methodist, the Christian's new birth in Christ is the realization of His pure love. It is a continuous process that takes place as a result of the indwelling of the Holy Spirit. Wesley uses the term

---

[327] Weisner, Andrew F. "Shaping Spirituality on a Lutheran College Campus." *Lutheran Partners* magazine. Available at http://www.lrc.edu/ministry/shapingspirituality.htm

[328] Wood, Laurence W. "The Wesleyan View." in Alexander, Donald L. (ed). *Christian Spirituality: Five Views of Sanctification.* Downer's Grove, IL: InterVarsity Press, 1988, p. 95

"Christian Perfection, to speak about the center of what the Gospel is all about, the act of being renewed in 'the image of Christ.'" Wesley maintained that "all justified believers are sanctified." [329]

Wesley uses the term "a second blessing" to refer to a way in which one can experience the perfect love of God. The Christian perfection he eludes to does not eliminate the human element. Although Christ has freed us from the power of sin, it does not free us from the consequences of sin in this lifetime. The Holy Spirit continues to work to purge and sanctify the believer from the power of sin and opens the door to the possibility of an honest and deeper relationship with Christ.[330]

## Pentecostal View of Spirituality

Pentecostal spirituality places stress on the *experience* of the Holy Spirit. For Pentecostals, the center of the Christian message is Jesus Christ, but what is particular to them is "the personal and direct awareness and experiencing of the indwelling of the Holy Spirit."[331] An important note in this regard is that the emphasis is not so much the experience *per se* as the Holy Spirit, who is thought to be experienced personally. This "experience" is held in contrast to the "mechanical sacramentalism of extreme Catholicism and the dead Biblicist orthodoxy of extreme Protestantism" according to one scholar.[332] Another scholar has noted that the Pentecostal answer to the question "Where is the Church?" is not given in terms of a message nor of a given structure but "where the Holy Spirit is recognizably present with power."[333]

Pentecostals tend to be wary of discussing "theology" or "doctrine" of the Holy Spirit, not because they are fundamentally anti-theological, but because they are concerned with elevating theology to a place of prominence. Although they would largely agree with the traditional definition of theology as "faith seeking understanding," Pentecostals want to ensure that the faith is not merely formal or intellectual and that it be profoundly experiential. In fact, because they have had some form of experience, they have little regard for theology or doctrine that does

---

[329] Wood, p. 96
[330] Wood, p. 97
[331] Rodman Williams, Ph.D., quoted in Williams
[332] James Dunn, quoted in Williams
[333] Bishop Lesslie Newbigin, quoted in Williams

**Although they would largely agree with the traditional definition of theology as "faith seeking understanding," Pentecostals want to ensure that the faith is not merely formal or intellectual and that it be profoundly experiential.**

not recognize or participate in some experience. They are "convinced that the shape and content of their experience, which they believe to be of the Holy Spirit, is essential to the life and thought of the whole church."[334]

Another important focus of Pentecostals is the coming of the Holy Spirit at Pentecost as a continuing event, one that is not merely a once-for-all event but rather is experienced daily. They identify themselves with the experience of Christ's followers on the Day of Pentecost, namely, that one is to be filled with the Holy Spirit in the same manner as those who were there on that Day. They often refer to this continuing event as "baptism in (or with) the Holy Spirit." Other terms that are used for this experience include "outpouring," "falling," or "coming upon" of the Holy Spirit, whereby the person is said "to be filled with" or "receives" the Holy Spirit. However, the term used most frequently is "Baptism of the Holy Spirit" because it better conveys the idea of the totality of the event (signifying that the entire person is submerged in, activated by, the Holy Spirit) and the uniqueness of the event (a one-time experience in the Christian life). Hence, their pneumatology is "centered in the crisis experience of the full reception of the Holy Spirit . . . . Pentecostal pneumatology emphasizes not so much the doctrine of the Holy Spirit as it does the doctrine. . .of the baptism in the Holy Spirit."[335] Other terms used for this experience include "anointing" and "being sealed with the Spirit."[336]

A further aspect of this experience for the Pentecostals is that it is distinct from and subsequent to conversion. Although this Spirit baptism may occur at the time of conversion, it has nothing to do with conversion and may occur at some time thereafter. It is considered a "second" encounter with God or "second blessing" in which the supernatural activity of the

---

[334] Williams, J. Rodman. "Pentecostal Spirituality" in *The Pentecostal Reality*, point 1. Available at http://home.regent.edu/rodmwil/pent3.html

[335] F. D. Bruner, quoted in Williams

[336] Williams, point 2

Spirit becomes active in the Christian's life.[337] Hence, conversion, often referred to as "regeneration," "new birth," or even "salvation," is quite different from Spirit baptism. In contrast to the teachings of other evangelicals, who stress conversion-regeneration and the receipt of the Holy Spirit by every "born again" Christian at the time of becoming a new man in Christ, Pentecostals believe that to become a Christian is one thing, and to be "Spirit baptized" is another thing altogether.[338]

Later classical Pentecostal teaching has tended to minimize or even disregard this second work of sanctification as a prerequisite to Spirit baptism, and the stress has been diminished considerably by the neo-Pentecostals. For the most part, today's Pentecostals speak of Spirit baptism as a second experience of God's grace, but for empowerment to witness rather than for sanctification. In this more recent approach, sanctification in its initiatory stage is considered to be included in conversion or a lifelong process that may or may not include Spirit baptism.

> For the most part, today's Pentecostals speak of Spirit baptism as a second experience of God's grace, but for empowerment to witness rather than for sanctification.

Pentecostals also understand the Holy Spirit as acting differently in the two events of conversion and "Spirit baptism": in the former, the Holy Spirit brings about conviction of sin and contrition of heart, and thereby unites the believer to Jesus Christ. In this approach, the Holy Spirit dwells *with* the believer, acting in various ways upon the individual's life, but with the event of Spirit baptism, the Holy Spirit comes to abide *within* the person.[339] In this latter event, the person experiences God's presence and power "breaking in or becoming manifest" and the person has a new sense of reality in faith, namely a "lively sense of God's presence, a rejoicing in Him, a freshness in prayer and worship."

The primary term is *power* or *empowering*, which includes the power to heal, to cast out demons, and to do mighty works.[340] Two other terms

---

[337] *A Handbook on Holy Spirit Baptism*, p. 10, quoted in Williams, point 2
[338] Williams, point 3
[339] Ibid., point 4
[340] Ibid., point 5

that are important in understanding Pentecostal spirituality, especially Spirit baptism, are *heart purification*, a term from the Holiness movement that refers to a second work of grace preparatory to baptism in the Spirit, and *yielding* or *emptying*, wherein the candidate lets go of all barriers so the Spirit may move freely into the void. In conjunction with these two prerequisites for "Spirit baptism" is the need for expectant faith, one that holds firmly to the promise of the Father that He will send the Holy Spirit.[341]

Finally, Pentecostals associate baptism in the Spirit and speaking in tongues, an event evident as the initial evidence of Spirit baptism in which the individual speaks in "other tongues." Because this form of language is unknown to the participant, it is considered to be the language of the Spirit, which transcends ordinary speech in an "overflow" of the Spirit in praise of God. [342]

## Reformed View of Spirituality

Reformed spirituality has been described as the "stewardship of God's gracious gift of a full and complete relationship with him, according to Scripture,"[343] and one that "places special emphasis on the subject of sanctification."[344] The core of Reformed spirituality is two-fold: divine grace and human gratitude.[345]

John Cooper, Professor of Philosophical Theology at Calvin Theological Seminary, identifies the key characteristics of Reformed spirituality as "dependent on God, Trinitarian, personally intimate, 'worldly,' comprehensive, and open.," an outline that will be followed herein.

### Dependence on God

With regard to one's relationship with God, the distinction is made between the *focus* placed on God by other forms of Christian spiritualities and the *dependence on* God that characterizes Reformed spirituality.

---

[341] Ibid., points 6, 7

[342] Ibid., point 8

[343] Cooper, John. "A Reformed Perspective on Spirituality: All of Life is the Lord's." *Reflections on Reformed Spirituality*. Calvin Theological Seminary: *Forum*, Spring, 2002, p. 3

[344] Ferguson, Sinclair B. "The Reformed View" in Alexander, Donald L. (ed). *Christian Spirituality: Five Views of Sanctification*. Downer's Grove, IL: InterVarsity Press, 1988

[345] Adams, Richard D. Reformed Spirituality. Available at www.warc.ch/pc

Whereas some of the other forms concentrate on one's own efforts to get closer to God, including devotional practices, praise and worship, meditation techniques, and advances in nearness to God, the Reformed approach considers "genuine spirituality [to be] a gift from the sovereign God, who generates it in us through his Word and Spirit. Our efforts at spiritual discipline are empowered by God and ought to express grateful stewardship of his gifts."[346] Our relationship is rooted in the invincible and unconditional love of God that is expressed "in a relentless solidarity with God's own creatures, initiated by God and mediated in the person of Jesus Christ, which so bonds us to him that we can speak of mystical union."[347] Dependence on God is central to Reformed spirituality, which is "funded" heart, mind, and soul by the sure knowledge that the initiative lies with God.[348]

## The Trinity

The doctrine of the Trinity undergirds Biblical piety, and whereas the creeds relate creation to the Father, redemption to the Son, and sanctification to the Holy Spirit, the broader teaching of Scripture is that the Triune God is present in all his works. Because the Son and Spirit are active in creation and the Father initiates redemption and sanctification, a spirituality that fully recognizes and appreciates these truths is Trinitarian. Cooper notes that this point may seem obvious, but that many forms of piety concentrate disproportionately on one or the other of the Godhead or on the earthly Jesus as He walked with his disciples rather than on the ascended Lord who is seated at the right hand of the Father.[349] Reformed spirituality, then, maintains a scriptural balance that recognizes the relationship of the individual to the Triune God.

## Personal Intimacy

Another aspect of Reformed spirituality is the emphasis on the personal intimacy one has with the Triune God, as distinct from the "personal relationship with Jesus" that is the foundation for some other forms of spirituality. Those in the Reformed church desire a warm, personal, relationship with God, but that relationship is seen in terms of an intimate, loving relationship with the Triune God. Cooper notes that the

---

[346] Cooper, p. 3
[347] Adams
[348] Ibid.
[349] Cooper, pp. 3-4

"assurance that we are children of the heavenly Father through the Son by the Spirit is our greatest privilege, security, and joy." [350]    A major metaphor in John Calvin's (1509-1564) writings that speaks to this intimacy is the Father as "the fountain of divinity within the triune relations."[351]

## "Worldy" Aspect

Reformed spirituality also has a "worldly" aspect, not in the sense that it focuses on the world more than on God or that it is diminishes the reality and consequences of sin, but that it aims at living life as God created it here on earth.  This form of spirituality celebrates the fact that God created us from the earth, blessed us with children, and has given us dominion over the creation as "God's image-bearers in his 'very good' earthly Kingdom."   To be human means that we are called to live in loving obedience to Him as his children and covenant partners.    Rather than *removing* us from life, salvation and spirituality *restore* it.  By embracing the "ordinary" and tending to avoid the "extraordinary," Reformed spirituality relates to God from within the natural context of human life, rather than seeking transcendence to supernatural heights.

> Reformed spirituality relates to God from within the natural context of human life, rather than seeking transcendence to supernatural heights.

In contrast to those forms of spirituality that consider mystical meditation or unusual charismatic gifts as the highest forms of spirituality, the Reformed approach is to follow the pattern of Scripture:  Reformed Christians use more ordinary, mundane, and natural ways to commune with God, namely Scripture, the sacraments, prayer, and worship. Similarly, ordinary, everyday life with God is recognized as being full of inspiring surprises and exciting possibilities of growth, creativity, and excellence, in contrast to the prevailing culture that is quickly bored with familiar things and seeks something that is new and "exciting" and offers a "rush" or "peak" experience.[352]

---

[350]  Ibid.
[351] Zachman, Randall C. *Reconsidering John Calvin*. Cambridge, UK, Cambridge UP, 2012, p. 9
[352]  Cooper, p. 4

## Comprehensive

Because Reformed spirituality appreciates the "worldly," it is comprehensive in its involvement of all of life. Spirituality is not limited to so-called devotional activities, but encompasses our relationships with others; it is vitally concerned with marriage and children, with being stewards of the earth, and with engaging in culture. Reformed spirituality emphasizes that we must serve the Lord in *all* that we do. It permeates and integrates all of life, based not so much on *what* we do such as eat, work, vote, and so forth as on *why* and *how* we do it. The *why* should be based on our love of the Lord and our desire to give him glory because we are grateful that He is renewing our lives. The *how* should be in accord with God's will as expressed in Scripture and in the good order of creation. Hence, all is done with a conscious thanksgiving to God so that spirituality encompasses all of life's dynamics and circumstances.

## Openness

An important aspect of Reformed spirituality is its openness in the sense that it is open to the adoption of devotional, liturgical, and life-disciplines of other Christian traditions. Recognizing that we all are part of the "holy catholic church" and that we all are in continual need for reforming, Reformed spirituality embraces aspects of other traditions that can enrich and fill some of the gaps in its own approach. The "worldly" disposition includes the inclination to adopt and reform those good things in the culture for God's glory and for one's edification, as they invigorate one's spirituality. Cooper puts it this way:

> As grateful stewards of God's gracious power in us, we ought to cultivate an everyday spirituality that is biblical, self-conscious in its historic identity, and intentionally open to the richness of the broader Christian tradition and the best of contemporary culture.[353]

## Sanctification

Reformed spirituality also is concerned with, indeed is based upon, the doctrine of sanctification, two features of which are central: "Jesus Christ himself is our sanctification or holiness . . . and it is through union with

---

[353] Ibid.

Christ that sanctification is accomplished in us."[354] Jesus Christ, as the "author,' "captain," or "pioneer" of salvation (Acts 3:15, 5:31; Hebrews 2:10, 12:2) has gone ahead of us to open the only way to the Father, and He brings to the Father in similar obedience those related to him by grace and faith. Reformed spirituality emphasizes that Christ *is* our sanctification, that He not only died for us to remove the penalty of our sin but that He is risen again and has been exalted in order to sanctify our human nature in Himself for our sake.[355]

> Reformed spirituality emphasizes that Christ *is* our sanctification, that He not only died for us to remove the penalty of our sin but that He is risen again and has been exalted in order to sanctify our human nature in Himself for our sake.

Nonetheless, sanctification according to Reformed theology, is not a mystical experience whereby holiness comes effortlessly; rather the individual is involved in the process as God gives increase in holiness by engaging one's mind, will, emotions, and actions. [356] Among those actions are mortification, the recognition of the continuing presence of sin in the believer and Scripture's exhortation to deal with it severely, without which there is no holiness; imitation of Christ, in the sense that Christians live their own lives with a clear awareness of the lifestyle of Jesus Christ, the only truly sanctified human; and self-evaluation, in which one must see oneself from two perspectives: that in each of us dwells no good thing by our own creation or nature, and yet in Christ, we have been cleansed, justified, and sanctified so that glorification has begun in us.[357]

**Four Means of Grace**

Reformed spirituality also focuses on four means of grace, those areas in which grace and duties of sanctification coincide.

• The first of these is the *Word of God*, which is to be hidden in our hearts and by which our lives are transformed. As the God-breathed "sword of the Spirit" (Ephesians 6:17), Scripture "has the power to instruct the

---

[354] Ferguson, p. 48
[355] Ibid., p. 49
[356] Ibid., p. 67
[357] Ibid., pp. 63-67

**126**

mind, introduce clear thinking, inform the conscience and conform us to God's will." Distinctive to Reformed theology is that the purpose of Scripture to instruct believersis seen as the central one. Because Scripture reveals how God intended humanity to be when he created us in His image, sanctification involves conformity to the moral law, which remains the standard of holiness for the believer. Both the preaching of the Word and the private reading and study of Scripture are key components of Reformed spirituality.[358]

• Another means of grace involves *the providences of God*, "not least of which are severe trials and afflictions."[359] Both biblical biography and testimony confirm that God's providences are used to mold one's character, and that affliction can serve as a divine beacon to those who have strayed from His divine purpose.[360]

• In addition to Scripture and divine providences is the need for *community*, for fellowship with other like-minded Christians. It is in the context of fellowship of the church that sanctification matures. Reformed spirituality involves the church as a preaching and suffering community, one that is a caring and praying body of Christians as well as a fellowship of pastoral care.[361]

• A fourth means of grace is found in the *sacraments*, seen in Reformed teaching as communicative signs that point us away from ourselves to Christ; they also are "a visible, tangible means by which he communicates with us and we with him. They display his grace and our union and communion with him."[362] They are never separate from the Word of God, nor do they provide sanctifying grace from Christ that is not available in Scripture, for it is the same grace that we receive, being the same Christ who is held out to us. They are a "fresh realization of our union and communion with Christ. They point us back to its foundation and forward to its consummation in glory." Hence, we have the Reformed understanding of the foundation of sanctification: union with Christ.[363]

---

[358] Ibid., pp. 68-70
[359] Ibid., p. 69
[360] Ibid., p. 71
[361] Ibid., pp. 71-72
[362] Ibid., p. 73
[363] Ibid., pp. 73-74

# Contemplative Spirituality[364]

An approach to spirituality that transcends denominational and religious barriers is the contemplative form, which is based on an ancient understanding that spirituality expresses itself in the three main ways of knowing, acting, and feeling, attributes associated with God by Christian philosophy.

## Three "Ways": True, Good, Beautiful

Christian philosophy associates each of these ways with God's attributes of ultimate Truth, Goodness, and Beauty, qualities that call people to the Way of the True, Way of the Good, and Way of the Beautiful. Each of these ways has expression in every individual but may find a greater expression than the others at any given time.[365] Each of these ways also can be seen as an authentic expression of love.

• The way of the *True* seeks to deepen love through understanding (based on John 8:32). Those who are drawn to this quality consider love of God and neighbor in the sense of an intimate knowing and clear understanding and are interested in theology, philosophy, and psychology. They desire thought-provoking sermons, are interested in discerning accurate meanings of Scripture, and rely heavily on intellectual understanding but also are open to intuitive insight and inspired realization.

• The way of the *Good* expresses love through action and doing the righteous thing, seeking to be of service and to promote justice (based on Matthew 25:40). People attracted to this quality are concerned with helping the poor, visiting the sick, peacemaking, and social action; they have a strong concern for morality and look to Scripture for moral guidelines and calls to action.

• The way of the *Beautiful* expresses love in the form of feelings and devotion (based on Psalm 42:1). Those who are drawn to this way are particularly responsive to sensory and emotional dimensions of the

---

[364] Crumley et al. All information for contemplative spirituality is taken from this article.

[365] From Crumley et al: "The original Hindu sources are lost in history, but we do know that by the time of Christ, the great Hindu philosopher Patanjali had compiled sutras that organized these ways coherently. Hindu systems also often include a fourth path, Raja Yoga, which focuses mainly on medication and other spiritual practices. In Christian philosophy, similar paths can be identified in Anselm, Aquinas, and earlier in Augustine."

spiritual life and are concerned with direct, sensed experience of relationship with God and others. They are drawn to praise, thanksgiving, and adoration and have a special appreciation of aesthetic and inspirational aspects of worship.

### Integration of the Ways

The assumption is that these paths will come together in an integrated whole as the individual grows in spiritual maturity. Nonetheless, most people are likely to be drawn more to one way than the others, and a person's expression of love is likely to change with deepening life experience.

One way of understanding this process of growth in love was proposed by Bernard of Clairvaux (1090-1153), a 12th-century monk. Bernard suggested a three-step process during which the individual begins with the "love of self for one's own sake" and tries to overcome problems and gain satisfaction in life through one's own efforts. Finding that this approach fails to provide what one desires leads to the second phase, which Bernard called the "love of God for one's own sake." At this stage, the individual recognizes that we cannot manage our life on our own and so we turn toward the Divine for help. This step often marks the beginning of a conscious, intentional spiritual life, and in one manner or another prayers are answered and the active grace of God is recognized in one's life. Somewhere along the path, one's focus shifts from the "gifts" to the "Giver" of gifts, and love becomes focused more on God's self; this third stage is called "the love of God for God's sake" and births a new and profound realization of God's goodness that then leads to the fourth phase, "love of one's self for God's sake."

An important note is that not everyone experiences the spiritual life in this manner. Also, most people's actual experience is far less linear than the spiritual models seem to indicate in their stepwise progression.

Because contemplation is always a gift that cannot be achieved by any method or practice, it is held in contrast to meditation, which includes all the practices and disciplines that one may intentionally undertake in the course of a spiritual journey.

# Contemplation

Contemplative spirituality may take these different forms, but it is always foremost about love, perhaps the most profound expression of which occurs in what has been termed *contemplation*. Classically, this particular kind of experience, one of loving presence that comes as a pure gift of God, usually occurs in the context of prayer. The sacredness of the experience is captured in the Latin roots of the word, *cum* ("with") and *templum* ("temple"). Because contemplation is always a gift that cannot be achieved by any method or practice, it is held in contrast to meditation, which includes all the practices and disciplines that one may intentionally undertake in the course of a spiritual journey. In the Christian context, the sense of contemplation as "loving presence to what is" has meant finding God in all things and all things in God. A representative is Brother Lawrence, the 17th-century Carmelite friar, who used the phrase "the loving gaze that finds God everywhere."[366]

Although the word *contemplation* has been used to describe especially profound qualities of prayer, it often is associated with silence and stillness, including a withdrawal from the world. However, the term means immediate open presence in the world whereby one perceives and lovingly responds to things as they really are; hence, contemplation can occur in very active and noisy environments as well as in quiet and still ones. This experience is given to us from time to time and, although it usually is short-lived, it can have profound effects. Among these effects is the encouragement to develop a contemplative *attitude* to the rest of life, also called *contemplative living*. This attitude involves "an acknowledgment that the deepest currents of our lives are 'God's business,' not ours."

## God's Omnipresence

Implicit in this approach to life is a deep and radical trust in God's presence and mercy based on at least four basic assumptions. One is that the spiritual life is entirely about love because God is love and we are created in and for love. A second assumption is that God is present everywhere and at all times, although we may not always "feel" His presence. God resides within each of us and in all creation, being closer

---

[366] Brother Lawrence of the Resurrection. *The Practice of the Presence of God.* Spiritual Maxims, Chapter 6, para. 31. quoted in Crumley, et al.

to us than we are to ourselves.   In conjunction with these two assumptions is that this divine presence in and with us is not static or inactive but is, instead, " a dynamic, continually moving flow that continually seeks goodness, truth, beauty, peace and justice.   God . . . stands ready at all times to guide us, to lead us in the dance of life.  This co-participation is an endless invitation" (based on Psalm 139:9-10).  The fourth assumption is that because God's true being and movements are essentially incomprehensible to our faculties, much of the contemplative life is cloaked in mystery.

## Anglican View of Spirituality

We come now to Anglican spirituality and the defining points that set it apart from the concepts of spirituality expressed by other members of the faith.  Anglican spirituality is rooted in the medieval Church and is an expression of the English Church by way of the Reformation. [367] In terms of Guthrie's categories (described above), Anglican Churches fall into the third grouping of churches.

The roots of Anglican spirituality go back at least to the era of Gregory the Great, who demonstrated an aspect of Anglican spirituality that has characterized it ever since:  "the tendency towards spiritual inclusiveness."  He advised the missioners he set out to conserve whatever they possibly could of customs and beliefs of those to whom he sent them to proclaim the Gospel of Jesus Christ.  As a result, some of the terms Anglicans use, such as Easter (for *Eostre*, the Anglo-Saxons' springtime goddess) instead of Paschaltide, and other customs reflect an attitude that was more than courtesy:  Gregory "had grasped a principle ever since known to Anglican spirituality-even before there was such a thing as Anglicanism proper: that the Holy Spirit is not confined by or to various churches, but rather 'blows where it listeth'(John 3.8)" [368]

> Although it is central to Anglican spirituality, being read extensively and regularly and serially in the office and the Eucharistic liturgy, it is not the basis of Anglican spirituality *per se*.

---

[367] Guthrie, p. 1
[368] McPherson, 1. Inclusiveness: the First English Church in Anglican Spirituality.

With the Reformation came the first English prayer book (1549), which was not merely a collection of devotions such as produced by many other churches, but was instead an outline of a comprehensive Christian way of life that was intended to be used not only for public worship but also for private, individual Christian experience — spirituality. By determining to conserve what was best of monasticism, rather than be "cleansed" of it as many other reformers were determined to do, Anglican reformers sought to extend the monastic vision to all Christians and to claim St. Benedict for the entire Christian community.[369]

Another clarification of Anglican spirituality involves the role of the Bible. Although it is central to Anglican spirituality, being read extensively and regularly and serially in the office and the Eucharistic liturgy, it is not the basis of Anglican spirituality *per se*. Guthrie notes that the Bible is "never, purely and exclusively, the basis of any spirituality, even spiritualities which would think of themselves as biblical" because it is always read in some context. For Anglicans, that context is the corporate, liturgical, sacramental life of the Church, which accounts for the fact that the basis of Anglican spirituality is the *Book of Common Prayer*, which belongs to both clergy and laity.[370]

**Incarnational**

When we examine Anglican spirituality, we must look at several key aspects that identify and define Anglicanism. First, Anglican spirituality has at its base the doctrine of the incarnation, and, hence, is *incarnational* in nature. Jesus Christ, the "word made flesh," is the full revelation of God. It is through the Person, life, work, death, and resurrection of Christ that we come to an understanding of God or, more correctly, an attempt to better understand God. God is more than we are ever capable of understanding, but it is through the person of Christ that we move close to that eternal union. Of the incarnation, Holmes remarks that it "embraces the totality of life. It is the doctrine which undergirds the Anglican commitment to sensibility, the openness to the entire experience with all its conflict and ambiguity."[371] Taking to heart the doctrine of the incarnation, Anglican spirituality emphasizes the goodness of the material world and sensuality as part of the creation of God, who took on

---

[369] Ibid.
[370] Guthrie, pp. 5-6
[371] Holmes, Urban T. *What is Anglicanism?* Harrisburg, PA: Morehouse Publishing, 2003, p. 29

human form. It emphasizes a sacramental view of the material world as a doorway to the divine, and at times tends towards the Orthodox doctrine of *theosis* or deification in the sense that it emphasizes our participation in the life of God and our ultimate goal of communion with God.[372]

As a central doctrine to Anglicanism, the incarnation means that sin cannot be explained by identifying it with matter or with the physical world; rather sin is rebellion against God, the refusal to serve with God as co-creators, partners in bringing to fulfillment his vision for creation, and the violation of the law. Because the incarnation embraces the totality of life, this doctrine is foundational to the Anglican commitment to sensibility and the openness to the entire experience with all its conflicts and ambiguity. The incarnation is a sacrifice, God's becoming a servant to be one of us, and Christ's Passion is the moment of fulfillment. When Jesus Christ cried from the cross, "My God, my God, why hast thou forsaken me?" (Mark 15:34), he 'was not merely piously reciting psalms: he was staring into the face of evil. It was an authentic cry of pain, that echoes around the world again and again, and from the supreme source of incarnation springs the hope of humankind."[373]

> The incarnation is a sacrifice, God's becoming a servant to be one of us, and Christ's Passion is the moment of fulfillment.

## Liturgical

Anglican spirituality also is distinctively liturgical, corporate, and sacramental. As such, the liturgical life of the Church involves participation by laity as well as clergy, by those with occupations in the world as well as those who live a monastic life. Anglican spirituality arises from the common prayer of a body of Christians who are united in their participation through physical presence, liturgical dialogue, and sacramental action. It also involves a means of corporate participation that involves times and seasons, offices and ordinances, and readings and sermons. In this context, participation is in and through Christ, with God present to and for human beings in history in this world, gathered

---

[372] What is Christian Spirituality? www.stjohnadulted.org
[373] Holmes, pp. 28-31

together across time and space.[374] Anglicans view the sacraments as "outward and visible signs of inward and spiritual grace." Through the Eucharist, we become participants in the life of God.[375] The ongoing, corporate, liturgical life of the Church is supported by private devotion and prayer and meditation on the part of individuals.[376]

## Contrition

Another aspect that John Booty noted is contrition, which is especially evident in the theological writings, poetry, and works of devotion by divines of the 16th and 17th centuries. Contrition is intimately tied to the "sacrifice of praise and thanksgiving" in Anglican spirituality, although its meaning appears to be misunderstood in more recent days.

For the divines of an earlier time, such as Hooker, the beginning of repentance was contrition, which is aroused in the beginning by God's grace. An inward grief involving a pensive and corrosive desire that we had done otherwise, contrition is understood to be a deeply felt affection that is a response to the mercy of God, "the divine love extended toward sinners." [377] Contrition is not a brief moment in time in which one repents for all of the events of life and has no need for further repentance, for contrition is more than an isolated act of piety. It involves newness of life, as well as confession and absolution; it is fundamental to a life-long worship of God and to service towards God, our neighbors, and the rest of creation. It "involves that attitude towards the self that suppresses and hopefully will eliminate the sin of pride. When the altar of the heart is broken in contrition it is thereby opened,

> Contrition is not a brief moment in time in which one repents for all of the events of life and has no need for further repentance, for contrition is more than an isolated act of piety.

---

[374] Guthrie, p. 4

[375] Collins, Kenneth. What is Christian Spirituality? Copyright 2003 by Wesley Center for Applied Theology, Northwest Nazarene University.

[376] Guthrie, p. 4

[377] Booty, John E. "Contrition in Anglican Spirituality: Hooker, Donne and Herbert" in Wolf, William J. (ed), *Anglican Spirituality*. Wilton, CN: Morehouse-Barlow Co., Inc., 1982, pp. 27-29

made available to the working of God's Spirit, open to faith, hope and love."[378]

## Mystical

Anglican spirituality also has a mystical element that is distinct from "pietism." In contrast to pietism, which refers to a spirituality that involves an acute, immediate, life-changing experience of God, mysticism as part of Anglican spirituality "sees the union with God as the end of an ascent, requiring discipline, purgation, study, emptying and patience." It looks beyond the things that are visible to the invisible reality of God.[379]

The mystical aspect is captured in the liturgy and the Eucharist. This liturgy, being a very ancient form, is God-centered rather than man-centered. The entire form—words, song, chant, color, incense, light, shape of the building—all are woven together into an artistic form that touches not only our minds but all the other senses. Liturgical worship is artistic, touching our emotions as well as our minds, and "focuses our attention on the 'awful' presence of Christ, through adoration, praise, thanksgiving, prayer and hearing of his Word. In so doing it makes real the spiritual reality of Christ's presence."

The most powerful means of promoting an awareness of the mystical union we possess with Christ is the Eucharist. The bread and wine are intended to remind us of His sacrifice on our behalf; as we "feed" on them, we are prompted to "feed in faith, to possess our Lord and be united with him The bread and the wine taken into ourselves are then signs of Christ's infusing presence within our very persons."[380]

Perhaps the best summation of Anglican spirituality is that offered below:

> The Anglican spirit was still, as it had always been,
> one which refused to separate
> The sacred from the secular,
> The head from the heart,
> The individual from the community,
> The Protestant from the Catholic

---

[378] Booty, p. 4
[379] Holmes, p. 66.=
[380] Findlayson, Rev. Bryan. "Mystical Union." Anglican Spirituality. Pumpkin Cottage Ministry Resources Available at http://www.lectionarystudies.com/pbspirituality.html

The word from the sacrament.

--Gordon Mursell

## Conclusion

As is clear from these different approaches and emphases, no one church or group has a corner on spirituality. Each has something to offer to the person who seeks a deeper understanding of God and one's relationship to Him. We must trust in the goodness and grace and mercy of God to lead each of us in this pilgrimage and to keep in mind the exhortation offered by Lisa Dahill:

> At the centre of all Christian spirituality is the Spirit of God in Jesus Christ, who continues to call, gather, enlighten, and sanctify the whole church and each Christian. Called and gathered Christians will continue their own personal and professional explorations in this powerful, numinous arena of Christian faith. Jesus promises us that the Spirit of truth will guide us into all truth (John 16:13). With firm, discerning, and joyful reliance on this ever-surprising and ever-faithful Spirit, we trust that we will not be led into untruth, however unfamiliar some of these new ways may appear. Along with Christians of many traditions, and indeed with those on earth in whom God is ever working in mysterious ways, we continue to have much to offer and much to learn — together.[381]

---

[381] Dahill, Lisa E. Spirituality in Lutheran Perspective: Much to Offer, Much to Learn. Word & World, 1998, 18(1):74 Available at
https://wordandworld.luthersem.edu/content/pdfs/18-1_Pop_Culture/18-1_Dahill.pdf

## Chapter Seven

# MINIMAL VS. EXPLICIT ARTICULATIONS OF THE FAITH
## A Comparison of The Articles of Religion and the Belgic Confession

The Church has had numerous articulations or confessions of faith over the course of its development. Two that stand in contrast to one another by virtue of their explicit or minimal statements are the Anglican Articles of Faith and the Belgic Confession. The Articles of Religion are to Anglicanism the essential statement concerning church doctrine and church practices. Taking positions similar to those of some of the great councils of the early Church, these Articles have "guided and guarded the Anglican Church for over 400 years" and "their status as the defining document of Anglican theology has not changed."[382] Growing out of the Reformation, the Church of England made clear its position on doctrine and polity using as its guides holy Scripture and the creeds that, along with the canons, had emerged from the early Church councils. What emerged from this distinctively National Church was the *Book of Common Prayer* and the Articles of Religion (hereafter called the Thirty-Nine Articles).[383] Another major Reformation document, which was finalized a few years before the Thirty-Nine Articles, was the Belgic Confession. Being the oldest doctrinal statement of the Christian Reformed Church, it consisted of thirty-seven articles that were not merely a revision of the work of John Calvin, but a completely independent composition. It receives its name from the region of the Netherlands that now is divided into the Netherlands and Belgium.[384]

---

[382] Pascoe, Samuel C. *The Thirty-nine Articles: Buried Alive?* Solon, OH: Latimer Press, 1998, pp. xi-xii

[383] Toon, Peter. "The Articles and Homilies." In Sykes, Stephen, John Booty, and Jonathan Knight (eds), *The Study of Anglicanism.* Minneapolis, MN: Fortress Press, 1999, p. 144

[384] CRTA (Center for Reformed Theology and Apologetics). The Belgic Confession. http://www.reformed.org/documents/index.html?mainframe=http://www.reformed.org/documents/BelgicConfession.html

## Historical Development of the Documents

Although the two documents, the Thirty-Nine Articles and the Belgic Confession, essentially address the same concerns of the Church with regard to Christian doctrine, faith, and sacraments, they are quite different in many respects, some of which will be addressed in this chapter. Many of the differences can be attributed to the historical, political, and social contexts in which they were written, and, hence, a brief history of their development is essential to gaining an understanding of the purposes of the different statements, as well as the differences in emphases, tone, and genre (namely, decree versus confession).

### The Thirty-Nine Articles

The Thirty-Nine Articles as we now know them evolved from a series of earlier documents. After the English Church split from Rome in 1534, the important documents or statements of faith appeared to define and articulate the position of the English church on certain conflicts at that time. The first of these statements were the Ten Articles (1536); the "Institution of a Christian Man" (1537), also known as the "Bishop's Book"; and "A Necessary Doctrine and Erudition for any Christian Man" (1543), also known as the "King's Book." The Ten Articles were drawn up by a committee appointed by King Henry VIII. They reflected Henry's religious views and tended to exclude what he considered extreme Protestantism. The "Bishop's Book" was the work of Bishops under Archbishop Cranmer, but it never had the authority of the King, Parliament, or a convocation. The "Bishop's Book" included an exposition on the Ten Commandments, The Lord's Prayer, the Apostles' Creed, and the seven Sacraments, and addressed the doctrinal issues of justification and purgatory.

In 1538, Archbishop Cranmer met with Lutheran and English scholars, hoping to arrive at some form of consensus among Protestants. This group drew up a document entitled "The Thirteen Articles." These articles were never published; the texts were uncovered two centuries later. Nonetheless, the document served as a clear link between the Augsburg Confession and the Thirty-Nine Articles.

The final statement of faith during the reign of Henry was the so-called "King's Book," considered by some Church leaders to be a regression to

Catholic doctrine. After Henry VIII died and the youthful Edward VI ascended to the throne, Archbishop Cranmer moved toward a more fully reformed position. In 1551, Cranmer drew up a book of "Articles of Religion."

The following year, a series of forty-two articles, based on earlier articles as well as the Thirteen Articles drawn up by the joint Lutheran Anglican consultation, was produced. The Forty-two Articles were ratified in 1553, just weeks before the death of Edward VI. With Edward's death, the Catholic Queen Mary ascended to the throne, and shortly thereafter Protestants came under severe persecution. Archbishop Cranmer was burned at the stake, and *The Prayer Book* and Articles of Religion became defunct. Not until after Queen Mary's death and Queen Elizabeth was in firm control of the crown did the Church return to its former Protestant stature (Settlement of Religion, 1559).

> The Thirty-Nine Articles ...were published in Latin and English and have remained unchanged for more than three and a quarter centuries.

In 1571, Bishop Jewel of Salisbury was charged with reworking the Articles of Religion. In that same year, the Parliament and the convocation passed the Thirty-Nine Articles. They were published in Latin and English and have remained unchanged for more than three and a quarter centuries. As a result of the 1604 subscription, all members of the clergy were required to assent to the Articles, along with the *Book of Common Prayer*.

### The Belgic Confession

The Thirty-Seven Articles of the Belgic Confession were primarily the work of Guido de Brés, a minister of the Reformed Church who later was to die as a martyr for his faith (1567).[385] The Belgic Confession was drawn up in the midst of religious persecution by the Spanish Catholic King Philip II, who controlled the low country. Although his father, Charles V, the King of Spain, had been somewhat tolerant of the Reformation, Philip, upon receiving the throne, viewed himself as the divinely ordained protector of Roman Catholicism. He was intent upon

---

[385] CRTA

squelching the emerging Protestantism, particularly in the Netherlands, which had a growing economic prosperity and independent spirit that appeared to threaten Spain and the monarchy.[386]

De Brés had traveled as an itinerant preacher in the southern part of the Netherlands, and in writing the Confession had as one of his purposes to prove that followers of the Reformed faith were law-abiding citizens who professed a true Christian doctrine in accordance with Holy Scripture (as opposed to the Anabaptists, who challenged the authority of the civil government).

> [The Belgic Confession] is considered "one of the best symbolical statements of Reformed doctrine."

The Belgic Confession was completed in 1561. On November 1, 1561, a copy was tossed over the wall of the castle of Tounay, the signers hoping that it would reach the king's commissioners and thereby prove them to be innocent of the charges of heresy and sedition.[387] The Confession was accompanied by an address in which the petitioners declared that they were ready to obey the government in all lawful things, but that they would "offer their backs to stripes, their tongues to knives, their mouths to gags, and their whole bodies to the fire," rather than deny the truth expressed in this Confession.[388] However, rather than being found innocent of heresy, the Reformed believers were judged guilty and suffered torture and death.

Although some theologians consider the work similar to or at least along the same lines as the Confession of the French Reformed Church, written primarily by John Calvin and published two years earlier, it is an independent composition. It was revised in 1566 at a synod held at Antwerp and adopted by national synods held during the last three decades of the sixteenth century. The text was revised again in 1618 to 1619 at the Synod of Dort, after which it was adopted as one of the doctrinal standards to which all office bearers in the Reformed Church were required to subscribe. It is considered "one of the best symbolical

---

[386] RCA (Reformed Church of America). The Belgic Confession.
http://www.rca.org/aboutus/beliefs/belgic/index.html
[387] Ibid.
[388] CRTA

statements of Reformed doctrine."[389]   In 1788, the Belgic Confession was translated into English by a committee of the Reformed Dutch Church in America.[390]

## Divisions of the Thirty-Nine Articles and of the Belgic Confession

The doctrinal purposes of the Articles set forth by Cranmer and others were to ensure that the Church of England was an apostolic church with regard to teaching the apostolic faith; to ensure that the clergy would be sound in their teachings, not exposing their congregations to unorthodox teachings; to foster unity in the church; and to establish "perimeters" of comprehensiveness, using the gospel as the foundation.[391]

The Articles can be divided into four major subdivisions based on themes, according to W. H. Griffith Thomas:[392]

(1)     The Substance of Faith (Articles I-V)
(2)     The Rule of Faith (Articles VI-VIII)
(3)     The Life of Faith, or Personal Religion (IX-XVIII)
(4)     The Household of Faith, or Corporate Religion (XIX-XXXIX)

Within the last grouping are four subgroupings:
(a)     The Church (XIX-XXII)
(b)     The Ministry (XXIII-XXIV)
(c)     The Sacraments (XXV-XXXI)
(d)     Church Discipline (XXXII-XXXVI)
(e)     Church and State (XXXVII-XXXIX)[393]

The Belgic Confession also has been divided, in this case, into seven major divisions:

(1)     God and the Means by Which He is Known (I-XI)
(2)     Creation, Providence, the Fall, and Its Consequences (XII-XV)

---

[389] Ibid.
[390] CRTA
[391] Toon, p. 146
[392] Thomas, W. H. Griffith. *The Principles of Theology: an Introduction to the Thirty-Nine Articles.* London: Longmans, Green & Co., 1930, cited in Toon, p 153
[393] Toon, p. 146

These particular divisions indicate a difference in the primary focuses of the two documents: whereas the Thirty-Nine Articles focus primarily on individual and corporate faith, conduct, and worship, the Confession focuses on specific doctrinal issues or points.

## Comparisons of the Contents of the Thirty-Nine Articles and the Belgic Confession

A point-by-point comparison of the two documents is beyond the scope of the present work, but comparisons of articles on key doctrinal issues, namely statements regarding God, the canon of Scripture, original sin, and justification by faith, serve as sufficient examples of the differences, particularly in tone and emphases.

### God
Both documents open with a statement regarding God and both address His attributes, but with distinct differences.

*The Thirty-Nine Articles* begin by presenting a case for the substance of faith:

> There is but one living and true God, everlasting, without body, parts or passion; of infinite power, wisdom and goodness; the Maker and Preserver of all things, both visible and invisible. And in unity of this Godhead there be three Persons, of one substance, power, and eternity: the Father, the Son, and the Holy Ghost.(Article I)

Clearly, the emphasis is on God's being one and true, reminiscent of the first of the Ten Commandments in which God declares Himself to be the only living God and alone to be worshiped, obeyed, and adored. This concept is emphasized further by mention of God as not only Creator, but Preserver, of all things, thereby invoking a relational aspect to His creation. The Article ends with a clarification of the Trinity: three in one — and of one substance, one power, and one eternity.

*The Belgic Confession* also begins with a statement regarding God, but it focuses on a basic statement of monotheism and a personal confession to such:

> We believe with our heart and confess with our mouth that there is only one God, who is a simple and spiritual Being; He is eternal, incomprehensible, invisible, immutable, infinite, almighty, perfectly wise, just, good, and the overflowing fountain of all good. (Article 1)

The language of the confessional statement is clear and to the point, with a catalogue of God's attributes. It is more elaborate than the first article of the Thirty-Nine Articles.

The two most obvious differences between the two articles is that, whereas they both emphasize that God is one and both provide specific descriptions or attributes of God, (1) the former is a didactic statement, whereas the latter is a confession of faith[394] and (2) the former makes a doctrinal statement regarding the Trinity, whereas the latter makes no reference to the Trinity. This is not to say, however, that the Belgic Confession does not address the Trinity. Rather, it devotes an entire article (Article 8) to defining and explicitly explaining the Trinity. Article 8 of the Belgic Confession begins by stating that God is "One in Essence," and yet is "distinguished in Three Persons." An elaboration of this distinction of the three Persons and yet one God states that God is of "one single essence, in which are three persons, really, truly, and eternally distinct according to their incommunicable properties." These Persons are named as "the Father, the Son, and the Holy Spirit." In addition, Article 8 distinguishes the Persons of the Godhead according to their relationships and/or roles: the Father is "the cause, origin, and beginning of all things"; the Son is "the word, the wisdom, and the image of the Father"; and the Holy Spirit is "the eternal power and might who

---

[394] This difference in tone will be true of all the articles, as the two documents are different genres; the Thirty-Nine Articles constitute a doctrinal statement regarding the Anglican faith, whereas the Belgic Confession takes the form of a personal (and corporate) confession or agreement with aspects of the faith.

proceeds from the Father and the Son." The Confession then qualifies this statement regarding their different properties by confirming that God "is not by this distinction divided into three" and is "but one only God."

Quite obviously, the Confession goes into considerably more detail in asserting and defining the Trinity, perhaps because the Thirty-Nine Articles were intended to be minimal in their requirements, as claimed by Bishop John Pearson in 1660.[395]

**Canon of Scripture**

> A traditionally recognized fact is that "for the Church, as for the Synagogue, the Bible has not only authority, but divine authority."

A traditionally recognized fact is that "for the Church, as for the Synagogue, the Bible has not only authority, but divine authority."[396] However, determining what constitutes the canon of the Bible involved a process and criteria upon which to evaluate various texts. The history of the canonization of Scripture is far beyond the scope of this work, but the importance of establishing the authoritative perimeters of any religion or faith cannot be overstated. Hence, both the Thirty-Nine Articles and the Belgic Confession delineate those books that are considered canonical, and both differentiate them from the apocryphal books.[397] However, the two documents take different measures in doing so. For instance, Article VI of the Thirty-Nine Articles articulates their relevance with regard to their "sufficiency . . . for salvation" and stipulates that "whatsoever is not read therein, nor may be proved thereby, is not to be required of any man," whereas Article 4 of the Belgic Confession is more concerned with

---

[395] Toon, p. 147

[396] Lienhard, Joseph T., S.J. *The Bible, the Church, and Authority: The Canon of the Christian Bible in History and Theology.* Collegeville, MN: The Liturgical Press, 1995, p. 4

[397] This distinction is an important note considering that recently the canon has been called into question, and assertions have been made that the apocryphal books were considered a part of the canon until the mid-1880s. See Lampe, Craig. *The Forbidden Book.* Goodyear, AZ: The Bible Museum (self published), 2004: "...the early church down through the ages, well into the seventeenth century, considered them [apocryphal books] Scripture and that the N.T. writers quote over 400 times from the fourteen books" (p. 31) and "They were translated from their original tongue into Greek and were part of the Septuagint. Furthermore, the Council of Carthage, in 406 A.D., canonized the books along with what we recognize as the rest of Scripture!" (p. 31). Of course, other controversies, such as those caused by Marcion and, later, Cyril Lukaris, explain the necessity of defining what one considers to be Holy Scripture.

defining them and their ultimate authority, stating that there are "two parts, namely, the Old and the New Testament, which are canonical, against which nothing can be alleged."

Both documents list in order the Books of the Old Testament, with the exception that the Article VI does not list the prophets, but merely states "Four Prophets the Greater" and "Twelve Prophets the Less" and does not specify Lamentations, whereas the Belgic Confession does. Another difference is the reference to "The first Book of Esdras" and "The Second Book of Esdras" in the Thirty-Nine Articles as contrasted with "Ezra" in the Belgic Confession.

With regard to the Apocrypha, the Thirty-Nine Articles states simply that "the Church doth read for example of life and instruction of manners; but yet doth it not apply them to establish any doctrine." A much more succinct statement regarding their status is made in the Belgic Confession, which devotes a separate Article (5) to state that "all these books" (Old and New Testament listed in Article 4) and "these only" are considered "holy and canonical, for the regulation, foundation, and confirmation of our faith." Yet another Article is devoted to listing the apocryphal books, and states explicitly that "we distinguish these holy books from the apocryphal." In comparison with the short statement in the Thirty-Nine Articles regarding their value, the Belgic Confession clarifies their status as being acceptable for reading and for instruction but that they are "far from having such power and authority that we may confirm from their testimony any point of faith or of the Christian religion; much less may they be used to detract from the authority of the holy books" (Article 6).

A major difference between the two documents is that whereas Article VI states merely that "all the books of the New Testament, as they are commonly received, we do receive, and account them canonical," the Belgic Confession lists the books themselves.

**Original Sin**

Article IX of the Thirty-Nine Articles and Article 15 of the Belgic Confession address "original sin" or "birth sin," but, again, the wording, and, hence, certain implications are very different. Clearly, Article IX is written to address a heresy, that of which "the Pelagians do vainly talk,"[398] and explicitly states that sin does not come from the "following of Adam" but is the "corruption of the nature" of every individual who is the offspring of Adam. Despite this clarification in the Articles, the Belgic Confession is even stronger, adding to the words that original sin refers to the "corruption of the entire nature of man and a hereditary evil" that extends to and "infects even infants in their mother's womb."

Likewise, although the Anglican Article IX uses strong terminology to describe the effects of sin, that the human nature is "inclined to evil, so that the flesh lusteth always contrary to the spirit" and "deserveth God's wrath," Article 15 of the Belgic Confession is much harsher and refers to it as "so vile and abominable in the sight of God that it is sufficient to condemn the human race."

Both articles are clear about the extensiveness of original sin ("every man" in the Anglican Article IX and "the whole human race" in the Belgic Article 15), as well as its persistence, although here again different nuances are noted: whereas Article IX specifies that "this infection of nature doth remain" after "regeneration," Article 15 states that it is "not abolished nor eradicated even by baptism." The implications in the use of "regeneration" and "baptism" raise doctrinal issues far beyond the scope of this paper but should be noted, nonetheless. Both Articles are clear that this nature does not impute condemnation to those who "believe and are baptized" (Article IX) or "the children of God" (Article 15), but the Belgic Confesion goes on to specify the means by which that is true—"by His grace and mercy [it] is forgiven them"—and further clarifies that such forgiveness does not give a believer license: "This does not mean that the believers may sleep peacefully in their sin, but that the awareness of this corruption may make them often groan as they eagerly wait to be delivered from this body of death."

---

[398] Pelagius denied Christ's provision of salvation and stressed man's ability to take the initial steps toward salvation by his own efforts, apart fromspecial grace; Jesus was seen as having "set an example." He was excommunicated by Pope Innocent I in AD 417. See Horton, Michael S. Pelagianism. Modern Reformation 1994, 3(1):26-32

## Justification

Considering that the doctrine of justification "stands above all other theological issues as the distinctive mark of the Reformation,"[399] one would expect that these two Reformation documents would have clear statements about it, and certainly they do. Of the thirty-nine articles, three are devoted to distinguishing between justification by faith and the merit of works; the Belgic Confession limits the topic to one Article (Article 22), but gives it no less space.

The former begins by stating the basis of justification as being on the merit of our "Lord and Saviour Jesus Christ by faith, and not for our own works or deservings." It goes on to state that "we are justified by faith only" and that this "most wholesome doctrine" should be a comfort.

Article 22 of the Belgic Confession also begins by stating that the basis of justification is by faith in Jesus Christ, but it is more explicit and addresses the work of the Holy Spirit, who "kindles in our hearts a true faith." This faith then embraces Christ with "all His merits" and seeks nothing other than Him. Apparently seeking to denounce teachings that attribute any efficacy to works, Article 22

> Hence, we cannot win or earn salvation through works; rather, good works follow faith in Jesus Christ.

stipulates that "all we need for our salvation" is Jesus Christ, that the "one who has Jesus Christ through faith has complete salvation," and that to assert that Christ is not sufficient and/or that something else is needed is "a terrible blasphemy."

After this critical doctrinal point is made, it is reinforced with the statement that "we are justified by faith alone, or by faith apart from works" and that "faith is only the instrument by which we embrace Christ our righteousness."

Article XII of the Thirty-Nine Articles also addresses the role of good works, defined as the "fruits of faith and follow after justification," and their acceptance to God in Christ, apart from having anything to do with putting away our sins. Hence, we cannot win or earn salvation through

---

[399] Weil, Louis. "The Gospel in Anglicanism" in Sykes, Stephen, John Booty, and Jonathan Knight (eds), *The Study of Anglicanism*. Minneapolis, MN: Fortress Press, 1999, p. 69

works; rather, good works follow faith in Jesus Christ. Another short article (Article XIII) explains the role of works before justification, namely that not only are they not pleasant to God because they do not spring of faith in Jesus Chrsit, but they likely have the nature of sin.

A most important addition to this topic is found in the last portion of Article 22 in the Belgic Confession: the imputation of righteousness. Building upon the statement noted above that "faith is only the instrument" whereby we embrace Christ, this article further explains that Christ imputes to us "all His merits and as many holy works as He has done for us and in our place" and that, indeed, "Jesus Christ is our righteousness."

## Conclusion

These comparisons of only a few of the articles demonstrate a characteristic that holds true throughout: whereas the Thirty-Nine Articles are "minimal in their requirements, leaving many secondary questions open," the Belgic Confession is considerably more detailed and explicit. The "minimalism" of the Thirty-Nine Articles, however, is by intent, as the writers sought not only to set aside troublesome views being propagated by the active sectarians, the traditionalist Romanists, and the growing group of Puritans, but also "peace in their attempts to provide straightforward statements of such doctrines as predestination and the descent into hell."[400] Hence, they are "incomplete in the same sense that the ecumenical creeds are also incomplete . . . . like the creeds, [the Articles] cannot ultimately be judged by what they omitted but by what they affirmed."[401]

For us, perhaps the most important consideration is that both documents were the works of faithful individuals who were determined to define and stand for the basic tenets of the faith.

*Departure from those tenets renders any position thereby heretical,*
*and we should be ever on guard to be as faithful*
*at protecting and fighting for the faith as were our forefather.*

---

[400] Toons, p. 147
[401] Pascoe, p. 58

# Afterword

In putting together this little book, my hope has been that it will serve to inform and encourage others in their faith. It is by no means extensive or exhaustive (is that even possible?) in any of the topics it addresses. Rather, it provides some insights gained from wise teachers, writers, and scholars and offers them to a next "generation" of students of Scripture. We stand on the shoulders of great men and women of the faith, many of whom gave their lives to protect it. May we be so faithful to ensure that the next generations inherit the "faith once delivered." In the words of the writer to the Hebrews:

*Now the God of peace, who brought up from the dead the*
*great Shepherd of the sheep through the blood of the*
*eternal covenant, even Jesus our Lord, equip you in every*
*good thing to do His will, working in us that which is*
*pleasing in His sight, through Jesus Christ,*
*to whom be the glory forever and ever.*
*Amen*

*Personal Notes:*

www.ingramcontent.com/pod-product-compliance
Lightning Source LLC
LaVergne TN
LVHW021501080426
835509LV00018B/2363